Identifying and Grieving Life

Good Grief

Ending Up in the Divine Embrace

By Dr. Nancy Moelk

Front Cover: Photo from the Garden of Gethsemane where Jesus may have prayed.

Other resources are available at firehouseminstries.com
Email: firehousemoelk@comcast.net

Contributions to or for the ministry are tax deductible under section 501 (c) (3) of the IRS code.

©Copyright 2017 Firehouse Ministries, Inc.
©Firehouse Ministries, Inc. 2003
©Firehouse Ministries, Inc. 2017
All rights reserved.

Table of Contents

General Introduction 3
Part 1-Good Grief 7
A Sovereign Furlough 12
Myths about Humanity 14
All Loss Must be Grieved 15
The Way of Truth 20
The Process of Grief 25
First stage – Shock 28
Second stage – Anger 29
Third stage – Sadness 32
Fourth stage – Bargaining 33
Final stage – Resolution / Forgiveness 34
The Cost of Delayed or Aborted Grief 36
Dying Daily 41
Conclusion to Good Grief 46
Part 2-Identify and Resolve Your Past 49
Life Patterns Emerge 49
How We Interpret Life Changes Everything 55
Our Cure Comes from Experiencing God's Presence 66
Short List of Unresolved Grief Issues 82
Bibliography 96

General Introduction

Identifying and Grieving Life Losses contains a set of tools for
- Helping people to see where they are repeating life patterns based on losses from the past
- To grieve those losses in a way that results in a deeper, more positive awareness of self
- To end up in a "Divine Embrace" with God in the Person of Jesus Christ as a result of this process
- An ability to offer self in personal relationships that are healthy and characterized by love

There are two parts to this set of tools which progress from the theoretical to the practical:
1. The theory of the grieving process as it relates to both God and man
2. The identifying of themes of life losses that keep repeating themselves

The first part is a detailed description of the grieving process. This process originates in the heart of God, who not only grieved His losses, but put the ability to grieve innate within the heart of all people by making them in His image. As we see what He is like and how we are made in His image, we are given permission and encouragement to embrace our losses by the grieving process. We then no longer must avoid them or express them malignantly to our own and other's harm.

The second part illustrates the types of life patterns that must be identified and then grieved. Telling stories of individuals[1] helps to teach the reader the language of the heart: how it tries to settle past losses by projecting them on to present day relationships.

My introduction to the idea that our past remains active in our lives came from a study of several people's work: the first being Dr. Mario Rivera; and then, Alice Miller, Dr. Daniel Goldman, and various periodical articles referring to the computer brain studies conducted on Romanian infants. Over the years, I have developed this idea both supporting it with Scripture and using it to help decipher the twisting of the human soul in its attempts to undo loss.

The concept of God grieving is something that I saw through my own study of the Bible over the course of many years. In as far as I know, it is an original insight concerning the Person of God and how it is expressed in humans, His creation made in His image. The stages of grief are based on the Kubler-Ross model as expressed in her 1969 book *On Death and Dying*. Although not every culture grieves exactly alike, all

---

[1] They are actually composites of different people I have helped over the years in my experience as a Christian prayer minister.

people on the planet go through some version of a grief process for significant life losses.

An article from the American Anthropological Association magazine, Ethos, documents the consistency of the experience of grief as well as the ability of our cultural expectations to modify the process:

> **The cross-cultural study of mourning offers promising ground for exploring the relationship between culture and emotional experience. Researchers have documented the profound feelings of grief, anger, and fear that accompany losses everywhere, suggesting that there is a "core grieving process" that occurs across cultures.[2]**

Accessing the innate grieving process within us and then steering it into an expression that leaves it resolved and us ready for life and relationship is the goal of our study. Addressing these issues, which can be a painful and difficult process, enables us to live a life of love.[3] Learning to love ourselves, others and God is a real possibility when we are no longer carrying around heavy weights of unresolved life losses. It frees us to use our energy to live fully engaged in the present. It

---

[2] Brison, K. J. and Leavitt, S. C. (1995), Coping with Bereavement: Long-Term Perspectives on Grief and Mourning. Ethos, 23. p. 395
[3] See Ephesians 5:2. All Biblical quotations are from the New International Version unless otherwise noted.

also allows us to be authentic about our true self since we have no need to be constantly managing hidden burdens of pain. I have seen these truths in action for over twenty years in my ministry and especially in the life of my family. **I offer this as a script for emotional health and transformation that is rooted in the Word of God: both written and in the Person of Jesus Christ.**

> **In Christian spiritual transformation, the self that embarks on the journey is not the self that arrives. The self that begins the spiritual journey is the self of our own creation, the self we thought ourselves to be. This is the self that dies on the journey. The self that arrives is the self that was loved into existence by Divine Love. This is the person we were destined from eternity to become—the I that is hidden in God, the "I Am."**[4]

---

[4] Benner, David G. The Gift of Being Yourself. (Downer's Grove, Illinois: IVP Books, 2004) 110.

Part 1-Good Grief

"Never does a man know the force that is in him till some mighty affection or grief has humanized the soul." – F. W. Robertson

Introduction

    A knock on the door at three in the morning is never a good omen. We were living in an immigrant neighborhood in Grenoble, France, the sole Americans among many Algerians, Moroccans, Tunisians and Portuguese. It was an unpredictable neighborhood in the day and not the type of place you wanted to open the door in the middle of the night. But when I peered through the peephole I saw my next-door neighbor, Fatima. She looked terrified and in great distress.

    Quickly I unbolted the door. She repeated the name of her five-month-old infant as if pleading with me. I followed her to her apartment and there on the bed lay her baby boy, his face a terrible yellow and gray color. I ran back to my apartment and woke up Gary. Within minutes he was speeding through deserted streets to the hospital with Fatima and her baby. The infant died shortly after their arrival.

    This sad episode in our missionary lives educated us to some of the elaborate grieving rituals in the Arab world. I was shocked at what I saw the next 40 days at Fatima's house. Every day women would stream through her door wailing and screaming at the top of their lungs. More than once I retreated to my apartment to put my head in my hands. I thought they were crazy and struggled to understand this strange custom.

    Now, many years later, I understand the wisdom of helping someone to grieve a loss. It can be the death of a loved one or a life event that has left them hurting and wanting. In fact, I see a greater significance in the grieving process – one that encompasses every facet of our lives and affects our relationships deeply. Recognizing and resolving these losses is the purpose of this book as well as understanding the origin of grief in the heart of God.

Grief, though painful, is a necessary step in recovery from loss. Some cultures are experts at helping one another through the grieving process. They help each other confront their losses and grief in a way that allows the mourner to go on with the rest of life fully after the losses have been sufficiently addressed. In addition to grieving death, older cultures provide outlets for other losses, as well. In some, young men are ritualistically dragged from beside their wailing mothers into the initiation of life as men. At the traditional Italian wedding, there is the "last dance" for the bride with her father and for the groom with his mother. I have seen many tears at these events during those dances. **These are powerful and important rituals that have been unfortunately discarded in our culture of disintegrating home and family life. Without them we are left with little opportunity to grieve the changes and losses of life.**

Both the Old and New Testament give examples of people grieving. In the book of Job as well as in other places, sitting in sackcloth and ashes was a way to express deep grieving. David openly grieved over the death of an infant. Samuel grieved over the removal of God's blessing from King Saul. Different prophets grieved over the sin and rebellion of the people of God. There was great mourning in Bethlehem after the horrible slaughter of infants, and at the tomb of Lazarus. Jesus wept over Jerusalem. Paul wept and grieved over the condition of the young church. James exhorted the people of God to grieve over their sin.

We are taught in our culture to avoid our grief and minimize the effects of loss on our lives. So, there is a problem for us in understanding the grieving process the way the New Testament church or the people of the Old Testament understood it. The grieving process was a regular part of their lives. Being "emotional" was considered normal when one encountered life losses. If there was a drought or if a marriage failed, the expected response was to be sad and to express grief. For biblical people this was a no-brainer. It was not necessary to explain grief to them: it was already deeply embedded in their hearts.

We glorify stoicism in our culture. People greatly admire Jackie Kennedy for not openly grieving the death of her husband. We consider it noble and dignified to hide our grief. Macho guy movies portray characters that slightly flinch at the deaths of close friends or family members. In a few minutes, they hop up and perform some heroic feat.

The choice to just be "in pain" seems crazy to most people in western society. We choose other options:

- We medicate.
- We stay busy.
- We shove it down.
- We try to forget. (To name a few!)

Unfortunately, emotions associated with our losses can't be forgotten. It may be possible to forbid ourselves from expressing feelings related to our losses, but they return to haunt us as headaches, fatigue, depression, illness, and unwarranted outbursts of irrational anger or anxiety. We trade tears for a deceiving web of symptoms. **One of the main tasks of Satan and his army of demons is to keep people from grieving. This especially makes sense when you consider that the end of the grieving process results in resolution of losses and forgiveness. The father of lies is an expert in encouraging denial.**

Until my thirties, I never contemplated what the "losses" in my life might be. I raced through my days without much thought of such things. Events and circumstances, which should have been counted as losses, were stiffly pushed aside. As a Christian, and particularly as a missionary, I did not believe I was supposed to be upset (for very long anyway) by anything. Here are a few of the losses I ignored (or tried to):

- We had virtually all our possessions stolen on our move to France beginning our 7-year stint as missionaries.
- Later, in multiple moves, we lost most of our things two more times.

- My mother rejected me for deciding to be a missionary and said she would no longer be a Christian.
- We lived under police surveillance.
- Believer friends were imprisoned and persecuted.
- People we thought we led to Christ turned on us and tried to hurt us.
- Other missionaries rejected us and tried to use us.

Such hardships I accepted as the cross I had to bear, period. I believed that to express my hurt and dismay over such things was to betray God and His provision. Unknowingly, I had carried over family and cultural patterns about grieving into my Christian life and imagined them to be "godly."

Years earlier, when my brother died at 24 years of age in a car accident, I couldn't stop crying. My mother gave me Valium for several days. Three days after he died, I was back in school. I remember walking through my classes in a fog all that year. When a teacher walked up to me and expressed his sympathy for my loss, I blankly looked at him and answered, "What for?"

Western culture is a stranger to grief, whether it is for death or for life changes. We even have multi-billion dollar industries that aid us in avoiding it. All kinds of medications replace simple tears or a bad mood. If anesthetics don't take the edge off, elaborate avenues of escapism will. Anything from movies …comfort food…shopping…to pornography and prostitution lay at our disposal.

It is no surprise that the world should run from pain. Pain is a sister to sin and its effects. A world in rebellion against God will not want to address such things. But what about the church? Does she welcome the mourner? Does she have the wisdom and strength to manage the process of grief from the losses of a sinful world? Maybe yes, maybe no. Many churches will allow tears of repentance and tears over the death of a loved one but these are tolerated in measured amounts: not too much and not for too long. After all, our loved one is better off now in heaven and we are to be rejoicing daily about what we have in Christ. **We are to present a happy face to the world that reflects our resolved and pain-free lives.** Sadly,

in the mistaken intention of presenting ourselves as an answer to the world, we have forfeited truth for appearances. Without a doubt, our culture's "feel-no-pain" mentality has influenced and deceived us.

Many years ago, I counseled several pastors. One thing I liked to ask them is how many sermons they have ever given or heard **on the effects of evil in our lives due to the sin of those around us.** Not one could remember such a sermon. Then I asked how many sermons they've heard on **our own sin and its effects.** You can be sure this is a favorite topic. Why so little on the suffering that evil produces in our lives through parents, grandparents, siblings, and friends, or society at large? Secondary to the forgiveness of sins, wasn't one of Jesus' main functions to experience the consequences of living in a fallen world? "The Father of compassion and the God of all comfort, who comforts us in all our troubles[5]," came here to know what it feels like to suffer at the hands of evil men? Does He shy away from our suffering due to evil? Are we to avoid discussing it?

In our performance oriented minds, suffering must have a "good point." Do we believe suffering for life's traumas, such as being unwanted or ignored by parents, laughed at by school mates, or passed over at the job--to name a few of the evils we may suffer--are allowed without being judged as "soft"? Like Pharisees who split hairs over nuances, we carefully arbitrate and pass judgment on which circumstances warrant a response of pain and for which we must stoically hide any reaction. **Out of touch with our true hearts, we aim for looking appropriate and maintaining image. We polish our masks and leave the misery of the inner self in solitary confinement.**

Christians from radically different ends of the spectrum do the same thing. Fundamental types retreat into head games and quoting Scripture, more charismatic types opt for flaking off into the supernatural as if they are on some drug. Our dilemma stems from a theology filtered by American culture. Although we have an

---

[5] 1 Corinthians 1:3b, 4a.

assurance that victory resulted from Christ's suffering at Calvary, we're disarmed by our own weakness, and feel ashamed of our own pain. Though we might know enough to desire to be broken before God, we stiffen at the first twinge of breaking. **In truth, we're ashamed of brokenness**. *Sure, we suppose it should hurt to pick up our cross. But it should never look like it hurts.* If we feel loss, we quickly conclude that something must be wrong with us. **With our concept of "the abundant life" slightly misconstrued, we actually miss out on a good deal of abundance by acting like we have it when we don't.**

What does it mean to pick up our cross other than to be willing to die to all that is not of God in our lives? Beside our own serious and widespread sins, we also have deep wounds caused by the sins of others. How do we die to the family losses of broken marriages that are so common in our society? Can we resolve emotional, physical and sexual abuse issues merely by addressing them with our cognitive abilities or avoiding them with feel good avoidance? Is it human to gloss over a life of rejection and isolation, pretending that such evils have no effect on how we view God and others?

We therefore, exist – many of us numb, many of us feigning joy and wearing a façade of strength, **and most of us oblivious to the conflicts buried within our souls**. The place where the reality bites is in our closest relationships: spouse, children, church, and work. We have fragile and shallow relationships where love is not sincere or strong. That's where I lived for many years.

A Sovereign Furlough

My husband and I had been missionaries in France, then Tunisia, and finally Morocco before my world came crashing in on me. When I became a Christian, I had believed that I was an entirely new creation, completely and perfectly transformed into one who would fully experience the power and love of Christ. And like everything in our culture, it couldn't be good unless it was "instant". I expected that I would walk in His peace, His joy, His patience now and forever…that the "old" me was dead and gone, and the "new" me would consistently grow into the image of Christ. Somehow, I thought that the prayers I prayed would be answered as I prayed them and I would not need to struggle again – that my problems were over! God began showing me that **much of whom I was prior to knowing Him was still very much alive and influencing my Spirit-filled life.** I had been delivered out of Egypt but there was still a lot of Egypt left in me. **The last thing in the world I wanted was to be in the desert for years. But as we know, that is where the Egypt in us gets addressed.** I didn't understand what was happening to me at the time, but God allowed several circumstances in my life to wear me down., They exposed some of the many hidden contradictions within me, and brought me to a place of surrender. It made me teachable.

Two things affected me deeply. First, while I was preparing to leave for the mission field, my mother reacted by rejecting me and threatening to reject her faith if I carried through with my plans. Confused and torn apart, I began my missionary life under a cloud. But I was committed to loving the people I went to serve, and nothing would change that.

Secondly, once submerged in the Arab culture, I gradually became aware of a sense of unease. Something I couldn't identify started to stir in me. I knew that something was wrong, but it was a while before I could admit to myself what I was feeling. My outward life, everything I was doing, every decision I was making said, "I love these people I came to minister to." Yet almost everything about Arab men repulsed me. Deep in my heart a voice whispered, "I hate these men." This conflict tormented me.

Instead of advancing in my faith the way I had expected, instead of becoming more victorious, more joyful, and fuller of love and peace and patience… I began sinking into depression and hopelessness. There seemed nothing I could do about it. With all my heart, I knew that God was true. Philippians 1:6 became my life's verse – "He who began a good work in you will carry it on to completion until the day of Christ Jesus." I would say that promise to myself repeatedly. Every night, unable to sleep, I'd get up to read my Bible and for hours I would pray, meditate, memorize Scripture, and make up little songs to comfort my heart. Despite all my efforts, I continued moving further into depression.

Finally, with the isolation of living in a land of scarce believers, constantly being watched by police, and having some of our believing friends put into jail for their faith, I could hold it together no longer. I couldn't keep up the charade. Though daily I taught the truths of the Bible to others, I wasn't seeing these truths impact my life the way I thought they should. I was pretending to be something I wasn't. While riding the crest of this conflict, with my hope at an all time low, I was sovereignly furloughed and soon to discover that I would not return to what had once been my life's call. I felt like a total failure. But being a failure had no place in my theology. It implied either God had failed or I was all wrong, horribly wrong, beyond redemption. I found myself facing a tremendous loss with no end in sight.

Myths about Humanity

Certain things about our nature just *are.* We were created by One much higher, a Master Craftsman who made us to His vision and desire. And just as the grieving process has been built into this nature, so, too the desire to be loved, to be known, to belong, has been written on our DNA. Irregardless of who we are or where we come from, whatever our personality type happens to be or even what birth defects might mark us as "different," we all have similar desires and needs. It's the basic package – the human condition, though marred, is still a divine reflection.

Because sin has penetrated our world, deception influences our lives, blurring God's established truths. Scripture tells us that Jesus came to give life... but Satan came to steal and kill and destroy[6]. Intent on keeping us from our Creator, he schemes to separate us from the truth. Thus, our world flourishes with illusions and delusions, a breeding ground for deceit and despair. Indoctrinated by our culture, we believe that we really don't require love... we don't need to belong... and that grief is both avoidable and

---

[6] John. 10:10.

unnecessary. Hidden behind our TV's, computers, endless activities, games, drinks and buffets, we hail independence, autonomy and emotional immunity. For the most part, we walk around mesmerized, like those in a cult convinced that right is wrong and bad is good. **Clueless about whom we are and what we need, masks are a necessity and fit us so comfortably we no longer recognize the self beneath.**

We reason, *I'm not going to sit around and feel sorry for myself.* This truly *sounds* good, but it, too, stems from illusions. Grieving does not include wallowing in self-pity or whining out of a victim mentality. We might assume people are grieving because we always find them in a depressed and mournful state, yet this is not the healing process of grief. Similarly, people with chronic anger, constantly resorting to backhanded ways to strike out at others do not model grieving either. These people portray conditions and lifestyles caused by their resistance to grief. If we vow, *I'm never going to be like them* and choose to avoid our pain, we ironically end up becoming like them.

Facing the truth about ourselves is not sin. Denying it is. Denial says that we're above needs and feelings. We pretend that our losses never really bother us because we're super-human. Truth is… there's only one type of human – the one that God made in His image.

All Loss Must be Grieved

What exactly is grief? The term *grief* refers to the range of emotions produced in a person after he has suffered a loss. In a world, devastatingly sinful, loss is unavoidable. All loss creates pain; and conversely – all pain results from loss. In other words, our pain universally and unequivocally points back to loss.

Though our losses come in all different shapes and sizes, we begin to understand them as we recognize that each fall into one of four major areas of pain – physical, social, emotional and spiritual. (I first heard this concept explained by Dr. Mario Rivera in an unpublished manuscript.) The breakdown of these categories helps us to identify characteristics common to our experiences. Within each category, the level of pain varies depending on circumstantial factors.

Physical pain is the simplest type of pain. It results from a loss of comfort in the body: the greater the loss of comfort, the greater the pain. Although physical pain can indeed exert acute discomfort, of all categories, it does not strike to the heart of who we are as much as the other three types of pain.

Social pain results from a loss of acceptance. When God created us, He said, "It is not good for man to be alone".[7] He understands our need for belonging. If denied acceptance in our social circles – whether these circles encompass our business world, church, school, or family – we suffer social loss and experience social pain. This pain varies in degree to the value or relevance the circles hold in our lives. A woman I know went to school every day as a child expecting to be spit on and ridiculed. The taunting words and unkind gestures of her schoolmates created manifold losses in her young life. Her constant fear at school threw her into a defensive posture and paranoia that deeply affected her adult relationships.

Suffering a breach in our nuclear family naturally creates the greatest social loss. Incidentally, our loss is real – *and must be dealt with* – whether differences separate us from our social circles, or our perceptions cause us to feel separated. If we feel like we're the black sheep of our family, our pain plagues us regardless if anyone else sees it from our vantage point. I grew up in a home where I was the only introvert among a family of extroverts. Because I couldn't relate to the interests of those around me, I felt as if I didn't belong. Because I didn't think that anyone attempted to understand me or share my interests, I felt excluded. Though these perceptions might exceed what I experienced, my social loss, nonetheless, stemmed from *reality* as I knew it.

Social pain diminishes in intensity as the group to which we long to belong increases in size. The pain remains substantial if shunned from our extended family. It continues as a factor in the

---

[7] Genesis 2:18.

realm of our town, state, and country. Many immigrants can recall coming to America only to be persecuted and ostracized. Despite the years that have passed since their trauma, they will attest that social pain on a national level can be quite severe, even debilitating.

But social pain also afflicts the person who feels embarrassed about his socio-economic status – that others look better, have nicer houses or cars, more prestigious jobs, etc… A child who has moved to a new city and speaks with an accent that distinguishes them from the other children causing them to feel that they don't belong, experiences social pain. Standing before a group of people and not knowing what to say, feeling the lack and resulting shame, reflects an episode of social pain.

Until the day I die, I will remember a day in 5th grade when I stood before the class to read a report. After three or four sentences spoken with my severe "s" lisp, the teacher complained to the class, "Let's get someone up here that can read!"

The next level of loss is in the emotional and psychological realm. We encounter this pain in our one-on-one relationships with "significant others." Emotional pain involves the loss of feeling loved or safe. Premier examples include death and divorce – the actual loss of the physical presence of a significant other. Any degree of disruption of these relationships due to sickness, travel, practical needs, or emotional unavailability creates emotional loss.

I work with many people whose parents got divorced after all the children left home. On the surface, it appears they need to address the pain of the divorce. But what emerges quickly is that the lack of harmony in the home was there for many years before the divorce. This created emotional and psychological losses needing attention as well. If discord threatens the relationships that comprise our "safe" environment, then it threatens us. The loss of a safe emotional environment causes emotional pain. We see this most visibly with children. Parents who constantly argue cause a tenuous and mounting sense of emotional loss for their children. Parents' relationships to their children are vital, but psychologists have determined that parents' relationships to each other have even greater influence on their offspring.

Jesus said, "Unless you turn and become like a little child you cannot enter the kingdom of heaven."[8] One of the characteristics of small children is their openness to being loved. They are welcoming and receptive to relationship and love. Jesus warned against causing these little ones to sin. One of the greatest negative lessons we teach our children is to stop being open to love because we have hurt them in their vulnerable state. **Not meaning to, we have taught them that love is a time when someone gets close enough to do some serious damage to our most vulnerable parts.** Unfortunately, I am speaking from experience here with my own four children. I have grieved much over my lack of sensitivity to them. I remember how open they were to loving me and receiving my love. I wasted so many opportunities in their early years to communicate love to them. Over the years, they have, of course, become much more cautious and guarded about letting me get close. I pray for them that God will open the gates of their hearts to His love as the perfect parent I could never be. I have asked them to forgive me for my failings and encouraged them to grieve these losses so they can find God in their wounding. I can't go back and repair the damage I have done, but my honesty about the evil I have committed against them will hopefully help them to resolve some of these things before they pass the evil on to their children.

Of all the types of pain to discuss, we find it easiest to talk about physical pain. Therefore, in church circles, we hear more prayer requests for physical ailments than anything else. Social pain requires a little more vulnerability – *No, I didn't have very many friends as a child… I didn't feel like I fit in… I was overweight and I talked too much.* This is harder to admit than – *I broke my leg when I was eleven.*

Our difficulty to authentically communicate our losses rises with the intensity of pain we experience. Emotional pain demands yet more vulnerability to express than social. Rare is the church group where people feel safe enough to share about family abuses and neglect. The tragedy of this lies in the disconnected nature of

---

[8] See Matthew 18.

most congregations. For many, the church becomes the new family. But with a heart full of unresolved patterns and conflicts ("the empty way of life passed on from our ancestors"[9]), this new family begins to look like the old one. Carrying around preconceived notions about others based on our ungrieved losses[10] makes for rocky and often short relationships. A few stay to duke it out, many continue their pilgrimage for the "perfect" church, which, as we know, does not exist.

Spiritual pain is the most profound of all. Spiritual pain, a response to the loss of harmony or communion with God, devastates our lives. We suffer spiritual loss more severely than any other loss because of its supreme and twofold nature. Not only do we need the One who created us more than we need our mother or father, home, reputation, or physical health, but He also is the source of all our provisions. Spiritual loss lies at the root of all loss. If it hadn't been for sin, no pain would have tainted our lives. Separation from God has cost us all, beginning at conception and weaving a web of losses through every nook and cranny of our life and times.

Though many of us have been born into a living, active relationship with Jesus at this point of our lives, to some extent, we still confront spiritual loss every day. If, while back in Eden, we had not suffered a loss of harmony with God – if we hadn't fallen away from Him through the rebellion of sin – pain would not exist. **All pain results from sin.** When He completely obliterates sin from our lives, so, too, will pain and loss, death and grief, fade into the archives of history. In this present life, however, sin thrives. Spiritual loss and pervasive grief remain inextricably tied.

Through the prophet, Hosea, the Lord says to us, "In their affliction they will earnestly seek Me" (v. 5:15). Per His design, every pain, every suffering exists as a vehicle to bring us closer to Himself, to cause us to know our God more fully, to understand His ways and to believe His promises for us. As only God can, He uses sin and its consequences – the very things that cause and define our separation

---

[9] I Peter 1:18.
[10] Later in this book we will take a detailed look at how we keep repeating relationship dramas until our losses are effectively grieved.

from Him – to draw us to Himself. From God's perspective, the goal of our pain is the restoration of our spiritual loss. Here, too, the converse is worth stating – addressing our spiritual loss through a greater intimacy with God consoles and brings healing to all our other losses. In fact, no other way exists to meet our physical, social and emotional needs. 2 Corinthians 1:4 reveals Christ as the preeminent remedy to the human condition – "(*He is*) the Father of mercies and the God of *all* comfort… who comforts us in *all* our afflictions."

When we are admonished in everything give thanks; for this is the will of God in Christ Jesus for you" it is not implying that God causes any and every evil thing that comes upon us. God does not sin. However, the reason we are to give thanks no matter what happens is that God is with us and will be able to turn every loss around into an opportunity to connect with Him more deeply. The grieving process is how this transaction takes place.

The Way of Truth

How, though, can we open our hearts to God, expecting and allowing Him to meet our spiritual loss, when our misconceptions about Him remain intact? **Through years of walking out of harmony with Him, we've incurred substantial loss of every kind. Thus, we have false beliefs that keep God out, and our losses unaffected by His healing touch.**

It was from this crazy arrangement that my problems as a missionary took hold of my life. Quite simply, I was not authentic. I had never been safe with anyone and I could not be safe with God. Intellectually, I knew truth, but I hadn't fully experienced it. In some areas of my life, it never penetrated. I said one thing, but in my heart of hearts, I believed another. Unfortunately, no matter how many times I said that I wanted to believe what I recognized in my mind as truth, these truths did not touch my unbelief.

From the time I was introduced to God and His Word, I assumed that I could decide to believe what I wanted. I then proceeded to build my Christian life *by deciding* to replace my quasi-truths, brick-by-brick, with His. It was mental: neat, quick, clean, and relatively painless.

But this proved utterly insufficient as well as impossible. "Jesus was a man of sorrows, acquainted with grief." Knowledge did not spare Him the pain of His losses any more than it could spare me. Through grief, Jesus came to resolution. Through no other route than embracing the full gamut of emotions created by His losses, could He forgive others and preserve the truth He had always known. "He learned obedience," Scripture tells us, "from the things He suffered"[11]. As Jesus allowed suffering to run its full course, He cultivated His countenance of humility and retained His character of integrity. The conflicts that plagued my soul could only be addressed in following His way: being a person of sorrow and acquainted with grief. Being "real" was the only path to true life.

If we observe small children, we notice that they grieve spontaneously. They might have a toy, for instance, and if that toy is taken from them, their first response is one of shock. Then they become angry, they start to cry, and they fight to try to take it back. If they can't get it back by force, they will likely cry for a while then return and plead for the toy. If this bears no fruit, they eventually give up and move on to something else. That's the grieving process in a nutshell – shock, anger, sadness, bargaining and resolution. It's automatic. No one needs to instruct them. No one needs to say, "Okay, now it's time to move from anger to sadness."

If a child experiences a loss, however, and doesn't have a safe place to grieve, the grieving process waits. **Sanctuary – feeling loved, safe and accepted – is essential to grieving.** Without it, the child will shut down and stay in the first stage: Shock/denial. More than likely, the child will recall his loss on an intellectual level, but his emotions will deny that anything has happened. If denial of loss is practiced on a regular basis, there will be a split in the child. Thinking will go one way and emotions will go another.

Once safe enough, the child's loss will resurface, bringing with it the natural emotional response. As the child grieves, his loss

---

[11] Hebrews 5:7.

heals, and the false beliefs associated with it will disintegrate along with the pain that created them. A friend of mine adopted a little girl as an infant. Before the adoption was final, the infant was given back to the mother temporarily and then permanently placed in my friend's home. One day, a few years after the adoption was finalized, this four-year-old child was watching an animal show on TV. During the show, she saw a wild animal with a litter of babies. For some reason, the babies were to be taken from the mother. At this point in the show, this small child became extremely agitated and upset. She ran to my friend and clung to her shirt crying, "Don't let them take the babies away from the mommy!" Repeatedly she frantically screamed this pitiful phrase. Fortunately, my friend had been taught something about the grieving process. She held the child close and reassured her that the babies would be fine. When the child had been quieted, my friend explained the story of adoption to her little girl. The child sat and absorbed this information, connecting her fear that had been stirred by the TV show to the fact of her own life. The truth was spoken in love to her fearful heart and she had peace at the end of her grieving. This simple but powerful moment with her adoptive mother will help to prevent great anxiety later in her life. **A few safe moments to grieve part of a loss: the world is a living hell without it.**

Make no mistake, though, until the time comes when a person feels safe enough to grieve, the loss waits, the emotions wait, the healing waits. Later we will demonstrate how life events that display any similarity to the hidden trauma can cause a perplexing over-reaction to current life situations.

It's not uncommon for children to reach adulthood still in a state of shock initiated in youth. Just as the little girl mentioned above was "triggered" by something she saw, we may be triggered daily to remember our losses. But we gloss over them, usually blaming others and ignoring the intensity of our reactions. Or else we suppress our emotions and hurry to say we have forgiven. Especially as Christians, we feel obliged to jump from offense to forgiveness in a single bound. That's the honorable thing, right? But loss without sounding out the pain and its emotions leaves little to forgive.

As adults, we rationalize, "Well, you know, Dad had a hard life. Mom was preoccupied. She had to work all the time." We push down the emotions from these losses, careful not to feel, continuing to pretend that any pain ever existed. The problem is, though, that it did. Somewhere within us, it still does. No amount of mental gymnastics can rewrite our history.

It's not that our parents were so bad. They may have been quite exceptional for parents. **The problem is that God is SO GOOD. And His perfect unconditional love is what our hearts were created for. Anything less leaves us with loss and pain that needs to be grieved.**

As hard as we work to suppress unwanted emotions, they fight to emerge. We exhaust ourselves contending with them daily through the course of our lives. Somehow, though, we're oblivious to the source of our exhaustion. We're blinded to the cause of our depression. We blame others for our chronic anger and discontent, for our repeated failures and trail of broken, or lacking, relationships.

The Bible tells us that God's Word is "truth"[12]. Not only that, but His word is "living and active and sharper than any two-edged sword, and piercing as far as the division of soul and spirit"[13]. We're promised that "the truth shall set *(us)* free".[14] We must understand, though, that we will only know God's truths at the levels we experience them. If we stay in the cognitive realm – merely believing but not receiving – our intellects may indeed receive freedom, but the rest of us will remain bound by confusion and fear. The greatest toll this takes on our lives, though, is in our inability to receive love (from God and others) and our inability to give love, particularly to those closest to us such as our spouses and children.

Resolving Ambivalence

---

[12] John. 17:17.
[13] Hebrews 4:2.
[14] John. 8:32.

When people or situations produce loss for us, it's typical to experience ambivalent feelings. Love and hate can be very close. We will often hate someone whom we need so much and who let us down. The hate stems from the disappointment of love. For children, these contradictory feelings appear irreconcilable. Unable to resolve ambivalence, they often decide to *make* a parent all "good" or all "bad". Their inability to acknowledge strengths and weaknesses residing side-by-side in one person causes them to record their past incorrectly. Many adults, as well, struggle in integrating the "good" and "bad" within others. In our tendency to idealize friends, spouses, siblings, and parents, being injured at their hands confounds us. Truly, only God is good. Everyone else will disappoint us and betray us eventually, even if it is simply by dying! We can't base our relationships on others' ability to provide what only God can give. Everyone in our lives is a bad person capable of good things and a good person capable of bad things. Refusing to accept the humanness of ourselves and others leaves us in a horrible idolatry and renders us unable to grieve effectively. To find restoration through the grieving process, we must break through the barrier of ambivalence.

Ultimately, we must confront such ambivalence about God. Paramount to reconciling our losses, we need to feel safe enough to wrestle with Him regarding our belief system about Him. We need to feel safe enough to say, *I feel a sense of loss, Lord, because I'm not 100% sure You want to take care of me. I had believed that my parents were gods, and I thought if only they would (fill in the blank)… I would be happy. I now realize that they were only human, and they couldn't. But You truly are God. You can! All along, You could! So, why didn't You?* If we resist acknowledging these emotions, we exclude God from answering the questions they raise. Somewhere deep in our soul, we answer them ourselves, but the conclusions we draw will not heal our loss. Instead, our false beliefs lay hidden from the light of God's Word, compromising its power in our lives.

How to Grieve is Coded Inside Us

No one needs to teach us to grieve, we already have "the code" written inside of us by God. However, there is something that must be in place for the grieving, which comes naturally, to go forward: sanctuary or safety. There must be, along with our sincerity, a non-condemning place to be honest. It could be called the way of truth, because it relies solely on truth to pull down deception and instill yet greater truth. It magnifies the fulfillment of God's promise, "and the truth shall set you free".

We all need a safe place to have good grief. Confession in its truest form needs to take place again and again. People need to express their anger towards a distant and cold father in one breath, and in the next they will need to weep over the guilt they carry at having done the same thing to their children and loved ones. Accepting God's forgiveness for sin is a short step from forgiving and understanding the parent who was once a victim, too. The hearts of the fathers turn towards the children and the hearts of the children towards the fathers.[15] True reconciliation and forgiveness come only after losses from evil are sounded out and embraced.

I used to think I was very tough and strong before good grief came into my life. I saw myself as being hard and able to bounce off whatever life dealt me. As good grief came into my life, I saw that it was this very same attitude in my mother that hurt me deeply. She seemed impervious to me, my needs, and my suffering as a child. To recognize the losses I suffered from her hardness was step one. Admitting the same hardness in me was step two. Facing the effects of my own coldness towards my children came next. Finally, I could conclude that I understood my mother and why she acted the way she did: it had been done to her as well. My heart turned to her. My heart turned to my children. Healing would be possible and the generational curse of hardness could be broken.

The Process of Grief

---

[15] Malachi 3.

Shakespeare said "Give sorrow words. The grief that does not speak, whispers the o'erfraught heart, and bids it break." If we were to map out our lives on a time line and mark when we came to know God, we would see a visual picture of all the points before that time when we lived unaware of His presence. God wants to meet us in every place of separation where we did not encounter His love. He desires to give Himself to us. In every disappointment, every cause of bitterness or resentment, He wants to soothe us and become the fulfillment of what we did not receive from this world. He wants to help us grieve so that we can become whole and fully consecrated and bonded to Him. The result of knowing we are enjoyed and wanted is a life that has an internal strength and joy independent of circumstances.

The person most interested in our healing is the Holy Spirit. Jesus said, "But the Comforter, the Holy Spirit, whom the Father will send in My name, He will teach you all things, and bring to your remembrance all that I said to you"[16]. Fortunately for us, He also promised to make His home with us forever. In other words, He works 24 hours a day, seven days a week to orchestrate events to open these areas and bring comfort and fullness to our lives. Some people, in their evangelistic zeal cry, "We need to forget about ourselves and get on with going to the nations." Should we send our crippled and diseased troops who will reproduce converts modeled after their broken and love-less lives? Having been a missionary, I know this too well.

I did not begin to address the great losses of my life until I was thirty-three. When the Lord led me to begin addressing them, I felt overwhelmed. Many hurts and losses surfaced, some taking me months to grieve completely. Some I grieved in a matter of a day. In the beginning, though, emotions of anger and hatred seemed to overtake me. I would wake up in the morning saying, *Ooo... I hate... I hate!* It wasn't something I invented at that moment. Years of vintage anger had surfaced, unassisted, from this deep emotional well buried within me. For the first time in my life, I felt safe enough

---

[16] John 14:17, 26.

to release them and give them expression. The Lord had convinced me – and *convicted* me – that those who "worship Him must worship in spirit and truth"[17]. This demanded that I honestly grieve my losses. Think about it: Did God know my emotions existed? Yes. Did I know? Not really. All the while I pushed them down, stiffening to suppress them; I had become increasingly hard and unreachable. I separated myself from myself, and wasn't truly available for Him, or anyone for that matter. Worst of all, I did this and didn't really know I was doing it. And to the extent that I did realize that I was burying my emotions, I believed I was doing it in obedience to God. My heart, deceitfully wicked, had me fooled about myself.

    I mentioned that I was ministering to Arabs in North Africa. My undoing began when I was confronted by my strong reaction of anger towards Arab men, the very people to whom I came to minister. My anger at Arab men stemmed from the terrible ways women were degraded in my own family. I had never faced my family's belief system or admitted my anger resulting from it. This anger greatly affected my ministry to Arabs and prevented me from loving them. But for years I didn't even know why I was angry. No amount of repenting or denying my anger made it go away. It was only by linking it to its point of origination in my original family that allowed me to grieve it. And it was only by grieving it that I could be released from it and be open to receive God's perspective about women, restoring and setting me free.

    I was in shock most of my life about the emotional, physical and sexual abuse that went on in my family. For me it was normal. I remember asking my husband one day, "If someone was hit in the head back and forth and pulled out of bed by the hair, would that be considered physical abuse?" Gary looked at me like I was joking and said, "Of course." I could never remember feeling the pain of the beatings. I remembered the shame of the rejection but had no memories connected to the physical pain. My body seemed to belong to someone else. It has taken me many years to reconnect to my body and the pain. It helped me greatly to know that Jesus

---

[17] John 4:24.

understood physical beatings and wouldn't run from me when I confessed how awful it was. Admitting it hurt was the first step to healing.

When we confront our loss, even in this numb, detached state, the grieving process begins. It proceeds to anger, sadness, bargaining and, finally, forgiveness and resolution.

First stage – Shock[18]

Shock is a natural response to pain and injury. In the moment of crisis, shock buffers us. Though reflex-like, shock is the body's way of protecting itself, a way of staying in ultimate control. Our pain is held at bay. As we release ourselves to the emotions of the grieving process, we relinquish this control. With each of the subsequent stages, we surrender a level of control in exchange for a level of pain. In this, God ensures that our emotions will not overwhelm us. Disassociation is a mental defense mechanism, like shock in the physical realm, which allows us to avoid mental pain and trauma. Disassociation can create the sense that we are detached from the suffering and observing the suffering of someone else. Unlike physical shock, which eventually dissipates after the injury occurs, it is possible to stay in a perpetual state of disassociation to avoid emotional pain. It is only when we can face our loss (i.e. becoming relationally safe) that our emotional shock will give way to anger.

A man came to me for help who had been adopted. He would joke about being left on the doorstep of a church. He couldn't admit that the abandonment by his parents had affected him. His reason for seeking help was that his second marriage was falling apart and he didn't want another divorce. It took some time, but he eventually came to see that although he had denied his anger and resentment toward his parents, he was now directing a disproportionate amount of anger at his wife and driving her away from him.

---

[18] The Kübler-Ross model, commonly known as the five stages of grief, was first introduced by
Elisabeth Kübler-Ross in her 1969 book, On Death and Dying.

Second stage – Anger

Imagine for a minute that we witness a mother screaming at her four-year-old child. *"You are so stupid! You spilled your milk! I should make you get down and lick that up like the dog that you are!"* How should we react to that scenario? Would it be normal to calmly defend the mother by stating that she probably didn't know any better… that perhaps she had "personal issues" which depleted her ability to cope? Honestly, is there a good reason to justify her behavior? On the contrary, something would be terribly wrong with us if that situation didn't cause us anger.

When we emerge from shock, anger naturally follows. In its proper place, as part of the grieving process, anger is cathartic. This emotion marks a milestone on our God-ordained progression towards healing. Many of us shudder and flee at the slightest display of anger. *Christians aren't supposed to feel angry,* a voice in our heads whispers. But who said? Doesn't God Himself experience anger over the acts and consequences of sin?

What about a child who's made to sit on the stairs from ten o'clock in the morning till six at night waiting for her father to come home to beat her? Or how about a boy whose father disciplines him by crushing his bare toes under the weight of his work boots? Shouldn't we feel angry with something like that? Why, then, when wounded souls such as these finally come out of denial should we expect instant forgiveness without any emotion?

A subtler but equally insidious sin against children is common in Christian families. The hidden justification for abuse goes something like this: *The way others perceive us as a family, and us as parents, is VERY important. The way you act when others are looking is far more important than how you feel or what you think. Wear a mask that protects our reputation as parents because this is valued more highly than who you are and the problems you might have.* We will likely never say these words. We might however communicate them by our actions to our children. To pretend that this is not evil denies truth. God indeed judges the heart. But parents rarely take the time to listen to what is in the heart of a child. Instead they insist that children perform certain behaviors and refuse to try to recognize the child's viewpoint.

I remember when my youngest was in kindergarten. One day he didn't want to go. I held him in my arms while he cried about having to go and expressed why he wanted to stay home. I comforted him in his sorrow but still made him go to school. He didn't get his way but he knew his sadness and anger were acceptable ways to express loss. Isn't God willing to listen to our anger and sadness tirelessly in prayer, affirming our feelings but still doing what is best for us?

"Be angry, and sin not," Scripture tells us[19]. Without question, it is sin to hurt someone, physically or verbally, to be vengeful, inconsiderate or malicious. Anger is usually associated with hurting others. Often it seems the person expressing the anger feels temporarily relieved and diffused, which is good for them, while they at the same time cause physical, emotional, or financial loss to others. Surely this is not the way to be angry and yet sin not. But how then should we express our anger? **What if we could express our anger in response to grief in a way that would serve to diffuse our anger, yet not hurt others?** We need

- To direct our present-day anger to its root cause
- To express our anger in a way that will not hurt others
- To correct the belief system from which the anger stems.

Let me explain this process with an example: a woman told me this story. Her four-year-old daughter spilled some rice on the kitchen floor. The mother, who had just cleaned up the kitchen, became emotional and angry. She scolded the child for her "thoughtlessness" and banished her to her room. The mother was perplexed about her strong reaction to such a minor, unintentional infraction.

We discussed the incident and her reaction to her daughter. Her anger was triggered by the deeply held, hidden belief that

---

[19] Ephesians 4:26.

children are not deserving of understanding and consideration, as well as the right to express feelings. Her own mother had taught her this. She had never been allowed to be angry with her own mother but now she had the opportunity to express her emotions freely towards her daughter. She was demanding her daughter give her the help and consideration she never felt she had received from her own mother long ago.

When this dear woman saw how she was unfairly dumping anger on her little one, she cried. I led her through an exercise where she admitted all that she had wanted from her mother, what she lost from never having received it and then agreeing to forgive her mother and seek the compassion and understanding she craved from a relationship with God in Christ Jesus.

The wounded child in each of us will continue to insist on payment from others, blaming them for our anger and pain until we recognize our losses and their roots. With good grief, we can resolve those losses and have God take over where others have failed us.

<u>It leads to sin to deny our emotions.</u> If we deny them, our pain remains unexpressed, buried, and dormant. It can be reactivated by some event that causes us to remember to some degree the original pain. We may not actually remember the event, but our memory, and original pain, is triggered, which then activates a whole series of emotions. We sometimes may erupt like a volcano or shoot off like loose cannons at our children, friends, co-workers or spouse, or worse, we lose complete awareness of our anger. In a passive-aggressive manner, we secretly release our unconscious hostility by tardiness, sloppiness, convenient forgetfulness, and side-handed ways to consistently convey anger towards everyone who somehow causes us to touch our original pain. Cynicism and sarcasm are disguised expressions of anger. Some of the funny people you know who always have a little jab for everyone may be angry but unable to deal with it directly.

It's far more constructive for a person to stamp their feet, let out a few bad words, yell and holler and admit they're angry than to behave like a Pharisee who essentially said, *I'm not angry, but I'll find a way to get back at you.* The Pharisees were full of passive-aggressive anger. They would never admit to Jesus: *You are threatening our political structure. We're angry with You because You look more important than us.* Perhaps it would have been their salvation to admit they were angry. Instead they said, *No, no, no, we're not angry. But let's just have a little meeting to see what we can do to rid ourselves of Him.* Cold and calculating revenge without ever having to confront their own hearts kept them from recognizing the One of whom their prophets foretold. **How about us? Will repressed anger hinder us from fully knowing our God?**

Third stage – Sadness

Sadness is the flip side of anger. It is more powerless than anger, closer to a full acceptance of loss. Sadness is simply, letting it hurt. Where anger causes us to feel powerful and somehow able to bring change, sadness is a relaxing of the fist. It is a sore and tender place of self inventory. After being angry for years over childhood abuse, a wounded person will move on in the grieving process when they finally stop fighting the past and embrace the tragedy of being overpowered and used.

One woman told me. "I have kept alive by staying angry. If I let myself cry, I may never stop. Somehow that seems like a defeat. To be so weak would be like dying."

Her wounded soul was locked in a terrible standoff. Her will to survive fought with her need for good grief. When she finally felt safe with me, the tears came. Her anger vanished and a well of sorrow replaced it. A side effect of her grieving these losses was the disappearance of chronic headaches that had plagued her for years.

Some add another stage of grief here: depression. It is a short lived, non-clinical depression. I believe it is the first confession of powerlessness on the way to forgiveness. Ultimate forgiveness can only come when we have ceased fighting off the loss and embraced the consequences of what has occurred. In short, it is learning to deal with reality.

I suffered clinical depression for many years. I was on medications. I used special lamps to try and raise the serotonin levels in my brain. I exercised, engaged in positive thinking, memorized Scripture, etc. Every month someone had another bright idea of how I could raise myself out of my depression. But there was no remedy for it.

When I started good grieving, the depression finally began to lift over time. For each loss that fueled my depression, I had to come out of denial. I touched the anger and sadness. Then I would usually suffer a few days of depression. But this depression was different. Instead of feeling like I was holding back a dam, it was a depression from an inner relinquishment of control. I had lost the battle to avoid pain. **It hurt but there was hope in it.**

The past cannot be changed. But our timeless God can turn the evil for good as we let go of our own solution and coping mechanisms. The depression in true grief is a critical turning point as we approach true forgiveness.

Fourth stage – Bargaining

The next stage, bargaining, is a place where our will makes a last-ditch effort to alleviate the suffering in our losses. Do I really have to accept this? Can't I work it out another way? I believe the deepest "deal" in all our hearts involves control and performance. *Surely there must be some way to make people love me. I will be acceptable by doing better.*

A man, Stan, who received ministry from me, kept on trying to get his father to understand him. His father had made it clear repeatedly that he was not interested in discussing their relationship. Stan grieved many losses concerning his father. For a period, he kept on returning to the same place. He kept trying to communicate his need to his father in a way in which his father would finally respond. He begged, he demanded, he reasoned, he challenged his father, but to no avail. Finally, he had to admit that he was beaten. He could never get the understanding out of Dad he longed for. Eventually he let it go, finished his grief, and could forgive his father. The result was that he accepted Dad just as he was and their relationship improved!

In his book, *Inside Out*, Larry Crab mentions our tendency to heap contempt on others or on ourselves rather than accepting that only God is sufficient. Bargaining says: I'll make it happen by being smarter, thinner, more loving, more spiritual ... you fill in the blank. Demanding the impossible from ourselves or others never resolves a thing. It sets us up for disappointment and resentments that weaken our relationships.

Often the spouse of an unfaithful partner knows the excruciating bargaining that follows oscillating episodes of rage and sorrow. *We'll make this marriage work by having another baby. It was just a fling. Our marriage is just fine. What could I have done differently?*

If we persist in trying to bargain away our pain, we settle into deceit, or magical thinking. Just like in fairy tales, we create in our minds an imaginary world. Like in all the stages of grief, when we refuse to embrace the pain and loss, we get stuck. Again, at this stage, only by God's grace can we accept the truth and move towards the freedom of forgiveness. "You will know the truth and the truth will set you free"[20].

Final stage – Resolution / Forgiveness

Matthew 18:35 warns us that our sins will not be forgiven, "...unless you forgive your brother **from your heart**." What is wrong with forgiving superficially? A lot. For one, if our forgiveness is superficial, we haven't let go of our anger and are still holding on to our loss. Secondly, we are deceived into thinking that the issue is forgiven and behind us. Forgiving from the heart, as we know, is not an easy matter. It is painful. It requires that we first resurface the original pain. It should not be surprising then that if we won't grieve, we won't be able to forgive from the heart.

Sounding out our loss through our emotions brings us to a clear, truthful state. The emotions are the smoke that leads us to the fire of our most inner belief systems. Because we're no longer hurt children, we can think as adults. With the repressed anger removed,

---

[20] John 8:32.

we can objectively look at the lives of those who hurt us and possess genuine compassion and understanding. This doesn't diminish what we suffered. But in that place of suffering and grief, in that vulnerable moment of honesty we have opened our hearts to God's presence.

Jesus Christ Himself comes and communes with us in our loss and disappointment. He restores our souls and gives us Himself where we had been clinging to a significant other. Knowing He is there, we can well afford to cancel the debt of those who have hurt and betrayed us. It is here that we move from knowing God in our head to knowing Him in our heart. Feeling the comfort of God directly in the place where you have been abused or scorned or forgotten is better than life. It is sweeter than the original abuse was bitter. It brings fullness where there was emptiness and companionship where there was loneliness. It causes the emotional cup of your heart to overflow with love.

My friend and co-worker, Richard was deserted by both parents at six months old. His grandparents dutifully raised him, but no one really wanted him. In his forties, he pursued knowing the Father heart of God with the help of a ministry dedicated to that. By the time I met him, he still had many grief issues to address, but there was an unusual strength in his character. It came from a deep-seated embracing of the truth that God had created him and wanted him no matter what his parents did. From there he set on the road to grieve the rest of his losses. The result was healing in his family relationships and a closer walk with God.

Like many who have been seriously rejected by their parents, his forgiveness of them has been a long process. Hurts that span many years are not quickly or easily grieved. There is a necessary sounding out of all the implications and results of complicated losses. How will we know when the forgiveness is complete? The greatest sign is a welling up of compassion for those who have hurt us. God's ability to forgive becomes a part of us. Our communion with Him feeds our soul, restores it, and causes an overflow.

This then enables our hearts to love others, even those that have hurt us. Now, we are free to forgive, and we can make that decision to forgive with integrity, in full view of the cost. Now our forgiveness will be authentic. It will not be easy but it will not be superficial. It will reflect our God's agonizing act of forgiveness.

After the resolution of God's anger, seen on the Cross, His relationship with man becomes based on what He can give to us, not what we can give to Him. When we grieve our losses, we come to the point when we no longer relate to others from the expectation of receiving. We cease to demand that others meet our needs and be what we want them to be for us. Our relationships become focused on what we can give. This giving flows out of the provision we have received of God's presence into the deepest wounding and disappointments of our lives. This is the kind of person who can live out the Sermon on the Mount. One who can, from the heart, bless enemies, turn the other cheek, and give without demanding recognition. These behaviors are not forced imitation but free flowing natural responses from the deepest part of our being.

The Cost of Delayed or Aborted Grief

As we have stated earlier in another way, the grieving process will unfold naturally unless something happens to make it stop. The lack of a safe environment almost always aborts grieving. Children from dysfunctional families usually do not grieve their losses during childhood because they don't feel safe enough to express what they're experiencing. Once safe again, which often isn't until adulthood, grieving can resume.

A friend in college, Jean, grew up with an alcoholic mother. Life with Mom was like living with a time bomb. Nobody knew when the bomb of her mother's rage would explode and injure an unsuspecting victim. Jean never grieved any of her losses. There wasn't room in the family for anyone else's emotions. Mom sucked up all the emotional energy. But years later when Jean married, it all came up. In the safety of her new home with a kind husband, the pent-up grief in her soul rose to express itself. She told me she spent several days on her couch alternating between rage and tears over the treatment by her mother. For a couple of months, she didn't speak to her perplexed mother. But after taking the time to get it all out and bring the losses to her heavenly Father, Jean could forgive. From there her relationship with her mother took a major turn. There was nothing to be angry about now; Mom no longer needed to repay her. Jean realized that her mother never had what she needed in the first place. In Jean's eyes, her mother went from being a powerful inflictor of pain to the needy lost soul who had no comfort for others or herself. In the end, Jean became a safe place for her mother to grieve. Jean led her mother to Christ several years later as the mother lay on her deathbed.

It is not unusual for us to cycle through the stages of grief more than once, depending on the depth of loss and the initial delay before the onset of grief. Normally, we continue cycling through the stages of grief until the issues are completely resolved. Sometimes, we repeat partial cycles of the first three or four stages until we're finally ready to move toward resolution.

Every time we handle our grief in a sinful way, we become stuck. It keeps us from God and the truth as we try to run away. It produces destructive behavior. Our symptoms will persist and augment. We may resort to some form of addictive behavior to medicate our pain. That's what often feeds extramarital affairs, pornography, prostitution, homosexuality, etc.

I am an expert at delayed grief. When we returned from the mission field I was an emotional and psychological wreck. But I still refused to consider good grief. I sought medical help from a psychiatrist. I was relieved to hear that I had a "chemical imbalance" and this was the cause of all my problems. This supposed that getting my chemicals in order would alleviate my symptoms. A few years and several medications later I was still depressed. So, I tried special lights. I would sit in front of these full spectrum lights for hours a day. Still, I got no results. During this time an elderly woman approached me and suggested that I may have some unforgiveness towards my mother. I was furious and curtly let the woman know she was wrong. "What a pushy person," I thought. "Just like my mother."

For many years, I thought my parents were faultless. The shock of the losses they created in my life turned into denial. My unwillingness to face my pain kept me in a state of untruth. Because I refused to be angry with my parents, my anger came out at others. My anger also came out toward myself. I couldn't let myself express this anger so I buried it somewhere deep inside myself. My depression was a by-product of the ever-present but unexpressed anger. It also manifested itself as a deep sadness that I couldn't express.

The bargaining that is part of grief can be a place where we get stuck as well. The chronic insistence that others make our lives right is truly magical thinking. The way we keep running from one self-help book or seminar to another implies we really think we are going to fix this mess ourselves.

Other evidence of being stuck in the grief process can be bitterness, resentment, hopelessness, and the lack of the desire to live. Some characteristics of good grief and impaired grief are listed below:

Healthy Grief
1. Shock
2. Anger
3. Sadness
4. Bargaining
5. Forgiveness/and Resolution

Impaired Grief
1. Denial
2. Chronic Anger
3. Chronic Depression
4. Magical Thinking
5. Unforgiveness / Recycle the process

Negative emotions, if not tended to, can cause psychosomatic reactions within a person's physical body. Conditions such as high blood pressure, heart disease, colitis, arthritis, asthma, headaches, and, even cancer can develop from the strain of attempting to hold negative emotions from expression and even awareness. Though these physical problems result from psychological issues, they are no less real.

Underlying feelings will find expression. Often, they manifest through defense mechanisms that significantly impair or interrupt relationships. As we've already seen, buried anger will eventually be displaced onto something or someone else.

Becoming stuck in one of the stages of grief causes depression, usually low-grade, but in some cases serious.

Sometimes people with bulimia or anorexia nervosa are stuck in the bargaining/magical thinking stage. They think that by not allowing themselves to eat, or by purging themselves, they will make their loss less severe, or will give them self-control over their feelings or over other people. We also sometimes make inner vows: we'll never allow ourselves to need anyone else, we'll never be sexual, we will always rescue others.

While we are in pain, our focus is on ourselves. We are, therefore, self-centered or selfish.

The answer isn't to address our symptoms, but to attend to the losses that create them. God wants to take us there far more than we want to go there. He is faithful, and everything He does to orchestrate our healing He does in love to bring us back to communion and harmony with Himself.

Because God is Spirit it's not enough to approach any aspect of our lives only in our mind. We must open ourselves completely to Him. If we so choose, we can pray rote prayers strictly from our cerebrum, and we can worship in like form; but God sees such acts as lifeless and of no effect. **If we desire for Him to will and to work in us, we must open our hearts without reservation. There exists no other way to resolve our losses than to let God enter authentic communion with us.**

There is a renewed interest in contemplative prayer. I once attended a one-day seminar at a local church to learn some of the techniques of this type of prayer. I was fascinated by the simplicity of the concept. We relax and present ourselves to God and His presence. In our state of rest, we contemplate a truth or word about Him. During that time things that contradict His truth rise to the surface in the soul before His presence. (His presence is truly a place of safety for the wounded soul.) God gives Himself and our souls receive what they need, and restoration happens.

Prior to practicing contemplative prayer, I received many hours of help from individuals who listened to me and tried to help me grieve. I am thankful for their help. It brought me a certain distance in healing. But since I have begun to sit silently in God's presence and let Him minister directly to my heart, I have seen deeper and more complete changes. I believe that both safe human and divine environments are important for good grief to take place. I am not against seeking human help--I work with people daily to help them with their unresolved issues. I am saying, though, that ultimately God gives us what we need, and people, however wonderful, will leave us wanting.

We are promised that if we are united with Christ in His death then we will also share in His resurrection. If we were to take a poll asking how many people wanted to be resurrected, the response would be nearly unanimous. If, on the other hand, we asked the same people how many wanted to die, no doubt, there wouldn't be many takers. The problem here is obvious. There's a requirement to the resurrected life – those who want it must die.

The apostle Paul, one of the first to understand this paradox, said, "I die daily." He explained to the Corinthian church, "We that live are constantly being delivered over to death… so that the life of Jesus may be revealed in our mortal flesh"[21]. To the Philippians, he expressed his chief desire, "that I may know Him, and the power of His resurrection and the fellowship of His suffering, being conformed to His death"[22]. The words of Christ had grabbed his heart – "If anyone wishes to come after Me, let him deny himself, and take up his cross daily, and follow Me"[23]. What is the Cross? It is the ultimate symbol of grieving. Paul knew that death comes before resurrection, and grief is vital to life. In Jesus' own words: "…for whoever loses his life for My sake, he is the one who will save it"[24].

When people are free to admit losses, others have visited upon them and grieve, an interesting thing happens. Suddenly their eyes are opened to the many ways that they too have inflicted pain and suffering on those around them. *I control my kids the way my mom controlled me! I have ignored my children like my dad ignored*

---

[21] 2 Corinthians 4:11.
[22] Philippians 3:10-11.
[23] Luke 9:23.
[24] Luke 9:24.

me. I never let others get close to me, I'm too afraid. I wonder if that is how my father felt, too? I have never heard a satisfactory explanation for Malachi 4:6 but I wonder if what we are seeing in the way of reconciliation here has something to do with it:

> **He will turn the heart of the fathers to their children, and the hearts of the children to their fathers,**

What becomes quickly obvious is that the evil that has been committed against us is a close sister to the evil that we perpetrate against others. The grieving process is the same for the losses we have caused in everyone around us. It is another crucial way that we must die daily.

Dying Daily

I have ministered to people who have been terribly abused or neglected. They come to me because they have not been able to find help. Most are Christians who are disturbed that their faith has not taken away their problems. A common stance is one of self-condemnation and self-hatred. They don't realize their ungrieved losses are twisting their perceptions. Too often they think God and the church have now become the abusive and neglectful family. This isn't to say that a person can't get beat up or used in a church system—but sometimes our view of people and situations creates a heavy filter that skews people's motives in our eyes.

One of the first things I do with people to whom I minister is to let them air their perspective on life and their relationships. With the guidance of the Holy Spirit, I help them to identify where the hurts originated and to grieve the loss of those earliest relationships. The next step is to help them begin to know God's presence in the place of wounding and to trust Him to provide the love, safety, acceptance, approval, etc. that was lacking. After this, they must begin to face how they have sinned against people in their lives and judged others for what they themselves have also done. The goal is to be able to know God's provision for their lives to the point that they can forget about themselves and live a life of love. By that I mean enjoying being loved and able to enjoy others. My early mentor, Dr. Rivera, used to put it this way: "One of the most important signs of health in a person is the ability to receive and give love."

I want to note here that the footholds of the enemy Paul refer to in Ephesians 4:27 are alive and well in the modern believer. When I lead a person in repentance, part of it is for them to renounce all cooperation with the enemy and his lies.

The same process of grieving that we use for resolving sexual abuse can be used for dying to our own pride and lust.

- We come out of denial about how proud we are.
- We may feel indignant and angry at first that God would show us this about ourselves.
- Next, we will feel sad that we aren't any better than the last person we may have judged for being proud. We had expected more from ourselves!
- In depression, we will begin to face our own powerlessness and how without His transformational power at work within us, we will never change.
- We may then try to bargain a little, questioning if this really is as bad as it looks and do we really have to let this go. Here we decide whether to give in to God's way of seeing our pride.
- Finally, we must fully accept the responsibility for our pride. We confess it and face the consequences of evil flowing from it. We admit that only God's Spirit can change our hearts, only He can restore our souls to God.
- Here we accept God's forgiveness and are reconciled to Him. Our repentance may involve many tears and a gut wrenching feeling in our stomachs. It won't be a painless, superficial head exercise.

We'll probably have to fight with ourselves to not try to blame others for our own sin. It is only by God's mercy that we can ever dare to face the many levels of sin in our hearts. It is only by God's kindness that we are led to repentance.[25]

It is through knowing God's unconditional love, His provision in all our suffering, His eternal promise of His presence that we can afford to humble ourselves and become servants of others. We can afford to pay the debt of love that we owe to all those around us. We can stop demanding others to make our lives right and instead start giving them of the riches of love God has shed abroad in our hearts. God will lead us to die daily to ourselves so that we may live in the power of His resurrection. He will lead us to die to such things as our devotion to the accumulation of wealth and things, our craving for recognition and praise, our selfish insistence on being right and having the last word, our habit of always putting our comfort and well-being above that of others, our own empire building, just to name a few!

From the safety of His love we will be amazed at how much evil we can admit in ourselves. We will progress, as Paul did, to seeing ourselves as a chief of sinners who has experienced unexplainable and immeasurable grace. It will become easier to feel compassion and to extend grace to others in their failings, having experienced deeply the patience and perseverance of God towards us in our many faults. Truly the one who has been forgiven much loves much![26] We become like Him in loving mercy.

Grieving our losses will move our Christianity out of our heads and out of the pews and into the inner being of our hearts as well as the lives of our children, spouses, extended families, co-workers, neighbors and friends. It will allow us to see ourselves and others as we truly are: broken people full of wounding at the hands of sin, desperate creatures separated from their loving Creator who crave without knowing it what only He can provide, dangerous characters whose evil poisons all those around them. "Ruin and misery mark their ways and the way of peace they do not know"[27].

---

[25] Romans 2:4.
[26] Luke 7:47.
[27] Romans 3:16-17.

Sometimes it seems that the church has unknowingly swallowed the American cultural mandate of "Doing is more important than being." Some church leaders will cruelly shout from the pulpit to their wounded flocks, "Get over your problems and serve God!" The implication is that if we start acting like we're healed, we'll be healed! This is unfortunately not true. It is manipulation by guilt at worst and serious denial at best.

They dress the wound of my people as though it were not serious. "Peace, peace" they say, when there is no peace.[28]

For this reason, missionaries and pastors fall like wounded soldiers in a heated battle. They give their all and when they are used up, the church banishes them in shame and disgrace. Often the sickest people in the church are the most active. They are desperately seeking Daddy's approval by trying to please the pastor and elders. Even though they give their bodies, so to speak, to be burned, they have not love.[29] God's love is something they keep hoping to be able to give to others but have never received for themselves. Is it any wonder that many have deserted the church for twelve step groups and self-help books?

Just add the church to the already long list of places where I give but don't receive. It just makes more demands on my already demanding life. You don't heal a broken arm by exercising it, my friends. It must be realigned and then protected from stress and strain. Once mended, it can slowly be used again and then move into vigorous retraining and exercise. You may be thinking, "This grieving process is too time-consuming. Surely God could not be orchestrating it."

Jesus spent thirty years being prepared for ministry, learning obedience through what He suffered[30]. Moses had a forty-year internship that began when he was already 40. Paul took eleven

---

[28] Jeremiah 6:14.
[29] 1 Corinthians 13:3.
[30] Hebrews 5: 8.

years of hidden growth before he began his ministry in earnest. Abraham was still having conflicts and learning from them in his eighties.

David was called a man after God's own heart. Did he have many conflicts with his family? His own father forgot to mention him as one of his sons when the renowned prophet visited his home. His brothers despised him and didn't see him as very important. In the Psalms David says things like, "Even though your father and mother forsake you, I will receive you." And "You knit me together in my mother's womb."

Now why do you think he said those kinds of things? Surely, he had wounding there, places where his soul needed to be restored. David married Saul's daughter, Michal, who then treated him with the same scorn as his parents and brothers. Did David pass on to his children his unresolved grief, treating them with the same aloofness and disconnect with which he had been reared? It appears he did. Did David seek to pacify his profound loneliness and isolation with an affair? Yes. David never resolved all his conflicts, but the psalms paint a record of his constant grieving: his facing his losses, his anger and sadness, his depression and bargaining and finally, at the end of almost every psalm his encounters with God. Such was the life of a man who was deemed, "after God's own heart."

Are we above these great people of faith? Is our American product going to be a fast and instant spirituality that defies the years necessary for maturation and depth? I don't think so. We can just continue in our proud denial at the cost of living spiritually shallow lives that look like massive leafy trees but which never produce any good fruit. (Note Galatians 5)

But the fruit of the Spirit is love, joy, peace, patience, kindness, goodness, faithfulness, gentleness and self-control. Against such things there is no law.

And as well:

If I speak in the tongues of men and of angels,

> **but have not love,**
> **I am only a resounding gong or a clanging cymbal.**
> **If I have the gift of prophecy and can fathom all mysteries and all knowledge, and if I have a faith that can move mountains,**
> **but have not love, I am nothing.**
> **If I give all I possess to the poor and surrender my body to the flames,**
> **but have not love, I gain nothing.**

Spiritual gifts, knowledge, faith, service, and sacrifice are all things that we do. They flow out of who we are. Who we are is intimately related to our losses and the losses we have inflicted on others. If we don't know God's love in these basic places of our souls, then we are lacking. What we do will not change who we are, only the communion of relationship both with God and others in our most vulnerable parts will transform us into the image of Christ.

Conclusion to Good Grief

So, the grieving process is part of picking up our crosses daily to follow Christ. **Jesus only had to die to all the losses in life created by the sins of others**. He had none of His own sin to repent of. **We will need to do both**. It is the same process for each. Here is a list of examples of how Jesus grieved:

- Jesus was shocked at the unbelief of the Jews.
- He was angry at their legalistic pride and greedy dealings.
- He was saddened by their history of rejecting God.
- He felt depression over the death and loss all around Him.
- He bargained by asking God if there was any way to avoid this way of resolving the loss of all the ages, but ultimately surrendered His will to the Father's.
- And then in a moment of great pain resulting from the consequences of sin and loss, He chose to forgive and He

understood that these clueless people had no idea how their evil was offending God and His creation.

We will follow this in many areas of our lives, for our sin and for the sins of others.

Just as there are many examples in the Scripture of people grieving, there are equally illustrations of those who refused to grieve. King Saul, when confronted with his sin by Samuel (1 Samuel 3), did three things other than grieve and die to his sin:

1. He pretended (denied) there was nothing wrong (vs. 13, 20).
2. He tried to shift the blame to others (vs. 15, 21).
3. He showed that his greatest concern was how he would appear before the people, not how his heart looked before God (vs. 25, 30).
4.

(I first heard this teaching on a tape by Bob Mumford many years ago.) Saul showed his insecurity in 1 Samuel 10:22 when he hid among the baggage. He demonstrated his control problem in 1 Samuel 13 when he decided to take things into his own hands out of his fear. Were these failings worse than David's? How did these transgressions compare to adultery and murder? The difference between Saul and David was not one of their degrees of sinfulness. David would have lost that contest. No, the difference between them was that David was willing to be honest about the contents of his heart before God and before the people. When confronted with his sin, David openly confessed before the people (see 2 Samuel 12) and wrote Psalm 51 to the Lord. He was familiar with the losses of his life and grieved them deeply. He was acquainted with both the effects of evil upon him as well as the evil he had inflicted on others. It is true that David passed on significant dysfunction to his children, but he left a legacy of how to resolve conflicts by facing those losses in truth and sounding out the depths of his grief, then knowing God in that place.

May God give us the desire for "truth in the inner parts" (Ps. 51:6a). May He give us humility to openly confess our rage, our disappointments, our fears, and our wounding in His presence at the risk of exposing our own failures. May He put us in a safe group of people who will not condemn our response to loss, but who will buffer our path through grief until our souls are restored and we live in His presence in every nook and cranny of our lives. May He lead us in service that is ordained and sustained by His resurrection power and not by our twisted drive to perform. May He bear much fruit in our lives that feeds everyone who is in relationship with us.

    I am convinced that God has put a blueprint in each one of us, a huge reservoir of potential that is just waiting to be discovered and developed. Grieving our losses helps to unbury the real person in there and to free them to be all they were meant to be!

    Now that we have investigated in detail grief, we need to look more closely at the ways unresolved grief issues show themselves in our daily lives. In part two, Unshackled From Your Past, we will use many examples from people's lives to demonstrate these patterns and how to trace backwards to the roots of losses that created them.

Part 2-Identify and Resolve Your Past

Life Patterns Emerge

Ruth had to sit down a moment to catch her breath. She still had the phone in her hand. The person at the other end had hung up abruptly. Ruth stared at the receiver wondering how a good friend could treat her so rudely. Ruth had recently joined a support group for divorcees and made a few friends. After a few months, it looked like the honeymoon in these relationships was over. The small group of women had turned on her like so many other former friends. Ruth had no explanation for it.

She turned her thoughts to work. Her supervisor at the plant was harassing her again, asking the impossible, she felt. After she left her last position she believed this would take care of the problems she was having.

For a moment, Ruth scanned a panorama of her life. Unhappy home life as a child, years of studying to be a social worker only to quit at her first position rather than be fired; a marriage ended in divorce, several churches joined and abandoned. The list of hopeful contacts and the ensuing ruined relationships was too painful to consider for more than a few moments.

A terrible thought sank into her heart like a cold dagger. What if it was something she was doing?

> **A plan in the heart of a man is like deep water,**
> **But a man of understanding draws it out.**
> **(Proverbs 20:5)**

Sometimes we are completely unaware of the reasons behind the patterns in our lives. When we keep repeating certain themes in our life situations, we are pursuing hidden and destructive agendas. It takes much wisdom and understanding to discern the reasons and purpose of our agenda. We formulate these secret agendas based on a series of losses from earlier in life. We internalize the trauma of our younger years, adopt it as normal, and create our world-view around it. No matter how crazy or unfortunate our life, it becomes a model of what we consider "status quo." From there, without realizing it, we draw people to us who are like our family members. we have unresolved conflicts with these people and try (without knowing it) to repeat our early drama, in an attempt this time, we believe, to make it work out. This is a way of trying to make our lives work. Unfortunately, it doesn't make them work; it becomes instead the fuel that helps destroy them. We are trying to map out our own way of saving ourselves and making ourselves safe.

> **For whoever wants to save their life will lose it,
> but whoever loses their life for me will find it.
> (Matthew 16:25 NIV)**

Does history seem to painfully repeat itself in your life, like in Ruth's? Even though her story is an exaggeration, a compilation of several people who have sought my help over the years, do you ever wonder why you feel stuck in certain unhealthy relationship patterns? Or wonder why things always seem to turn out disappointingly the same? Like a hamster on a wheel, you keep running along the same path and can't get off?

Are there certain "trigger" situations in your life in which someone says or does something that pushes a button inside of you and sets in motion negative reactions, feelings and behaviors? Do you get out of one crazy-making relationship just to fall into another?

The Scripture says that we reap what we sow. One application of this concept carries over into our perceptions and how we react to situations and other people. It would imply that we carry a hidden set of perceptions into every relationship, into every situation.

For over 25 years, I have worked with people and seen plenty of confirming evidence for the presence of destructive patterns in their lives. Helping them understand when and why they were triggered to repeat patterns and/or do destructive things proved to be a gateway to healing. The first step was admitting their part in the drama. The second step was the grieving process, which lead them to resolution and new behaviors.

The degree of healing in their lives depended on three things:

1. They could accept the reality of the losses that were creating their reactions.
2. They could effectively grieve their losses.
3. They could come to know God's provision instead.

Before they received healing, they were bound to their losses. They needed a key to unlock them from their losses and repeating the destructive patterns over and over. Our goal is to be unshackled from our past and connected instead to Jesus Christ.

Ruth's life demonstrated this sorry pattern of replaying the losses many times. Was it just coincidence that her relationships followed a similar course whether at home, work, or social life? Could it be that she carried inside a way of viewing herself, her world, and her friends? As her life unfolded she seemed to be interpreting each event and reaction through a filter in her heart. Her vision affected her reactions because she saw circumstances based on experiences in her past.

One of the writers who helped me deepen my insights into the dilemma of destructive and repetitive life patterns was an internationally known psychoanalyst, Alice Miller. She had practiced psychoanalysis for over twenty years only to resign when she discovered that addressing the traumatic losses of childhood could heal patients rather than symbol-laden psychoanalysis. In the Afterward to the Second Edition of her book For Your Own Good, she says:

For some years now, it has been possible to prove, through new therapeutic methods, that repressed traumatic experiences of childhood are stored up in the body and, though unconscious, exert an influence even in adulthood. In addition, electronic testing of the fetus has revealed a fact previously unknown to most adults—that a child responds to and learns both tenderness and cruelty from the very beginning.

In the light of this new knowledge, even the most absurd behavior reveals its formerly hidden logic once the traumatic experiences of childhood need no longer remain shrouded in darkness. (Emphasis mine.)

Many books based on brain studies confirm these teachings. Dr. Daniel Goleman speaks about a part of the brain called the amygdala which rules over what he describes as "Emotional Intelligence."

Whereas these studies focused on the more traumatic occurrences in childhood, I saw while ministering to people, that even small losses strung over the years of childhood were leaving their imprint on people's lives. Even people with "good" parents were reacting to losses of some kind or another. What then is the solution? How do you help people get over their losses that may date back as far as the womb itself? Everyone needs to have God give them what was denied. Each person is created by God with His love set as a default, anything less creates losses more serious than we ever let ourselves admit.

Let me explain. God crafted our inmost being with the idea that we would have a twenty-four hour a day, seven days a week relationship with Him. He designed our hearts to receive His unconditional and unfailing love. He meant for the people surrounding us to be unbroken vessels of His love. That is what leaves us so vulnerable, sensitive and open as infants. There is no protection against evil because it was not part of the original plan for our environment.

But, of course, we aren't born into Eden. Instead we appear in a womb of a human who has fallen short of the glory and purposes of God. From then on, our relationships may be well-intended but still fall short of what we were created for.

The losses in Ruth's life began early on. She had been the youngest of several siblings. She was never close or well liked by any of her siblings. Her mother would give in to her demands but at the same time scorn her and berate her as inferior. Her siblings resented Ruth's neediness dominating the family system and tolerated Ruth's presence but did not enjoy a relationship with her. This resulted in Ruth behaving as a bully, insisting on having her own way, but perceiving herself as a victim who was being bullied by others.

Ruth was reaping perceptions and wounding that had been sown in her life early on. Ruth had become a professing Christian in college and had an expectation that all should be different in her life now. She knew she would go to heaven when she died. But life in the meantime hadn't changed dramatically—as she had hoped. Ruth was suffering from "unresolved grief issues".

Unresolved grief is produced by any type of loss in a person's life which has never been properly expressed and resolved. When we speak of losses, most people think of major life events such as a death in the family, bankruptcy or other traumatic happenings. Yet there are many losses, small losses, which constantly plague our days here on earth. Because we are created to receive perfect love from a perfect Heavenly Father, our journey here on earth where we are separated from that perfect love is riddled with pain and loss. The imperfect human love our parents give us creates many losses from the time we appear in our mother's womb. Added to those losses are our own choices which have a destructive result.

David, the Psalmist, was aware of the need for an appropriation of God's presence in the womb. Ps. 139 declares God's presence with him there. I do not believe this was poetry. I think it was a transformational experience for David to encounter the truth of God's love for him and presence with him all the way back to his conception. David was practicing the presence of God for his past. Psalm 22 has a more poignant and painful rendition of this need.

> **Yet you brought me out of the womb;**
> **You made me trust in you even at my mother's breast.**
> **From birth I was cast upon you;**
> **From my mother's womb, you have been my God.**
> **Psalm 22:9, 10**

Such an encounter with God is what Ruth needed to repair her life's revolving door of conflicts and relational problems. An application of the presence of God not just for each of her present moments, but wherever the past bombarded her present with perceptions and attitudes that were formed apart from God's presence, this is what she needed to transform and heal her life and to equip her to love with God's love.

How We Interpret Life Changes Everything

One easy way to illustrate unresolved grief is to interview several different people about how they interpret the same situations. I had the opportunity to do this for several years while I worked for an organization where I ministered to numerous volunteers. Sometimes, I heard about the same problematic situation from several different people. I often knew about their childhoods from my relationship with them. It was not difficult to see their "unresolved grief" play itself out in each person's picture of the problem and how they reacted to other's actions and words.

For illustration purposes, I have created a hypothetical situation where our friend Marcy is at the lady's prayer meeting at church and she asks for prayer because she has felt very tired and discouraged lately and not much like being with anyone. There are five other women at the meeting. To demonstrate my point, let's project what some of the possible perspectives might be to Marcy's request for prayer:

Marcy says, "I need prayer. I have been very discouraged. I just feel like staying home alone and not talking to anyone. Getting to this meeting was a real effort!"

And here are five plausible responses from the five different perspectives of the women in the prayer meeting:

Juanita: "Poor Marcy! She probably has been doing too much with her family and at church. I'll make sure not to bother calling until she feels better. I wonder if I have been calling her too often?"

Mary: "That Marcy is always feeling sorry for herself. Poor me! Poor me! Why doesn't she grow up? That makes me so mad."

Rose: "Wow! Marcy always looks so together. I didn't think she had any problems! That must be embarrassing to share like that! I'll try to act like I didn't notice."

Sharita: "I wonder if she feels that way because of the argument we had last week about the kids making too much noise during the service. She probably feels like I don't like her anymore."

Tiffany: "I'll stop by and see Marcy tomorrow. Sounds like she needs someone to talk to. That's a terrible way to feel."

Why does each woman react to Marcy in such a different way? The answer lies in a perception filter that each woman carries inside. These filters were created by experiences in their pasts, some which were negative and created losses in their lives. Without even thinking about it they are following their own rules of relationships. From there they react to Marcy with what each believes is an accurate response to the situation. We can analyze each response and guess what losses, if any, in each woman may have produced such reactions to Marcy:

Juanita will ignore Marcy assuming when people are burnt-out they prefer to be left alone. Something in her background taught her that going off alone to lick your wounds is safer than making yourself vulnerable to others while in need.

Mary will scorn Marcy, demonstrating her own rule that to be weak and needy is shameful. Somewhere she has probably been treated with disdain when showing her own weakness. This reaction reflects the way she treats herself in such a circumstance.

Rose projects her own need to hide behind a "happy face" onto Marcy. Maybe Rose was taught to keep her chin up and pretend nothing was wrong as a way of coping with loss. Such a fake and unauthentic posture is a great loss itself.

Sharita will try to fix Marcy by taking the blame on herself for Marcy's problem. Her reaction demonstrates some loss that encouraged her to blame herself in trouble. She can control her universe by always being responsible for everyone's feelings.

Tiffany tries to console Marcy in the way she has been comforted many times by those close to her, beginning with her mother. She, like the others, offers that which she has received. In her case, it is positive, based on positive rather than negative experiences.

This is just a small slice of each women's life so we can examine it. Sometimes we will have a healthy response to people, other times we will respond out of our unresolved grief and hurt them with the same loss inflicted on us.

Each of these women has a history of experiences that have formed their belief systems. Out of that belief system they evaluate what Marcy has communicated and then react to their perception of what they believe she is trying to say and, then, act upon it. Each woman's response can be traced to past experiences. If each woman was willing to address their root conflicts, it would be possible for them to change their way of thinking, and, therefore, their reaction to Marcy.

Praise be to the God and Father of our Lord Jesus Christ, the Father of compassion and the God of all comfort, who comforts us in all our troubles, so that we can comfort those in any trouble with the comfort we ourselves have received from God.
2 Corinthians 1:3-4

As Christians, the goal for responding to people is to respond as a representative of God and His love for that person. 2 Corinthians 1:3-4 tells us that this happens when we receive from God and then, in turn, we offer what we have received from Him to them. To see them through His eyes and not our own perceptions is what we want. But our own experiential filter, full of unresolved grief, clouds our vision. Others receive what we have received. And if what we have received from our own families is still deeply rooted in us and has never been supplanted by what the heavenly Father must give, then our earthly heritage will be passed on to others rather than our heavenly heritage.

So, what would happen next in the interactions between our prayer group and Marcy? Let us focus for a moment on the next level of interaction in this situation. As each woman reacts to Marcy, then she will ingest the other's responses, interpret them based on her own perception or filter, and then react accordingly.

I have broken down into slow motion a process that takes place continuously and simultaneously. Before long the webs of perceptions, reactions and responses get so thick and entwined that it is very difficult to follow what is happening. It is obvious why our relationships can become strained so quickly at home, church and work.

Other recent studies of the brain have confirmed these phenomena. Due to the technology, which enables scientists to view and follow brain patterns in living subjects with the help of computers, we now see that emotional responses are embedded in a non-thinking area of the brain which can be triggered by the slightest reminder of a past event or relationship.

I experienced this triggering of emotions at a baseball game with my family. Two men sitting several rows in front of us began to argue and shout at each other. I immediately began to tremble and sweat profusely. My chest tightened and I felt weak. At the time, I was unaware of the reason for my reaction. In retrospect, I realize the incident was triggering in me fears created by a terrible fight I saw between my half-brother and father when I was a child. Their fight involved more than shouting. They hit one another and police came to our house. That day my half-brother was sent away to live with my grandmother. Although the men at the game were not people I knew and even though they never came to blows, the shouting alone was enough to trigger in me the whole emotional reaction from my childhood.

I needed to "process" these feelings through my understanding in a way that caused me to realize my reaction was not in tune to the present-day situation but one that belonged to something in my past. To accomplish this I had to grieve the loss of seeing two people I loved deeply try to hurt each other. I had to grieve the overall lack of harmony in my family as well as the loss of my brother's presence in my life. We had been close.

A present-day trigger to the brain calls forth a packaged response based on another time and place in the person's life. The whole scenario of the past event need not occur. Only a few similarities are necessary to trigger the brain's automatic responses to a past event. Although these studies concentrate on the simpler cause and effect of these phenomena by isolated events, I believe this pattern holds true for long term life circumstances as well as short term. In other words, long term neglect can have the same residual effect as sporadic abuse.

One day when Andrew, our son, was around five year's old, Gary, my husband, decided to teach him to ride a bike. As I watched this momentous event from the window, I began to feel afraid and out of control. One part of my brain wanted to stop Gary from teaching Andrew to ride the bike. I felt panic as if something dreadful would happen to Andrew on that bike. At the same time, another part of my brain was saying, "It's OK. He is going to be fine!"

At that point I could have done several things. I could have forbidden my son from riding that bike. Or, I could have gotten angry with my husband and accused him of pushing our son to perform beyond his years. I could have stuffed the whole thing and developed a headache. Or, I could have questioned why I was responding in this way and begin to investigate my own reaction.

Fortunately for my son and husband, I decided to do the latter. When I took the time to think about my feelings, I suddenly remembered the first day I learned to ride a bike. I practiced until I felt confident enough to try rolling down a hill. I pushed the bike to the top of a hill and with great excitement began a rapid descent.

Whether it was the newness of the experience or the thrill of speed, I don't know, but as I approached the bottom of the hill, I suddenly discovered I couldn't remember how to make the bike stop! I had put so much attention towards getting it to go, I had never thought much about making it stop. At the bottom of the hill I wiped out, fortunately with no greater injury than scraped knees and legs. But the incident represented a deeper injury to my person that left no visible scars. It only emerged later in a fear of heights and now with the uneasiness I was experiencing watching one of my children learn to ride a bike.

I felt out of control the day my bike sped down that hill. To say that incident with the bike was the only time I felt my life whirling out of control would minimize one of my important early life "themes". Habitual "out of control" situations in my life like sexual, physical and emotional abuse created an atmosphere where a wild bike ride didn't heal with my skinned knees. Instead it became a symbol in my brain of a life pattern. It is easy to see how people develop severe control problems and seek to take charge of everyone's feelings and choices around them. The cure for such control problems is not to find people who will let you dominate; rather it is to identify the profound feelings of powerlessness and lack of control which created the unresolved grief in the first place. Our losses have two sides, one involves the evil done to us; the other involves the ways we have cooperated with that evil and gone on to perpetrate it towards ourselves and others.

A close friend of mine grew up in a very nice family. There were no shouting matches or hidden abuse. The politeness of family members reminded me of British nobility at tea time. But my friend, Bruce, didn't appear to be living up to his potential. He had great ideas and a wonderful work ethic but everywhere you looked in his life you noticed one thing: here was a guy who was habitually overlooked. He was treated as a workhorse who would get the job done. He was used to performing tasks far above his pay scale but never recognized or rewarded appropriately.

When he came to me for help we decided that he was doing the work of someone getting paid twice his salary. As we talked about his childhood we saw a pattern emerge of him being overlooked. Although his home life was very safe, stable, and orderly, there was little relational or emotional connection. There was little to no recognition of his talents and abilities, or how he was different from his siblings. In brief, he was neglected.

So long as he cooperated with what was expected, no one spent much time or effort finding out what he thought or how he felt. His active mind developed all types of fantasies where he was noticed and appreciated. But the reality of his life never became any of the fantasies. Instead, each job he found seemed to lock him into the role of a minor character, always hoping to have more impact, but seemingly hidden from the notice of his colleagues.

Not surprisingly, he repeated this pattern in the churches he attended. He was quickly identified in that setting as a reliable person who could be counted on to do things, and not make any demands. He always had a place, albeit unnoticed, in the groups in which he was involved, but his heart longed for the responsibility of being a leader. After some ministry time, together, we uncovered this pattern. Bruce has since begun to stand up and be heard at work and church in a way he had never done before. He got a promotion in his company and before long ended up in leadership at the church.

The unresolved grief in Bruce was centered on his view of himself, inherited from the significant people in his childhood. He saw himself as a quiet, proper, and well-mannered person who didn't make many demands and worked hard to keep others happy. He lost out on the opportunity to develop his own ideas and direction when he settled for being mommy and daddy's little obedient child. I am not down on obedient children, but abject compliance from a child is not as healthy as it looks. Some of the most confused and wounded people I have helped over the years are the "compliant children" who spent their lives trying to keep mom and dad happy or the family together. They have suffered a terrible loss of never being themselves, but just a projection of what someone else wanted them to be. Another way this "compliance" injures a person is from the perception in the child that they are taking care of the parent by keeping him/her happy rather than feeling the flow of care coming from parent to child. This is a sick type of role reversal, even if it is only in the way the child sees his/her life. In other words, the parents may not be demanding or expecting at all that the child take care of them, but inside the child a set of perceptions and reactions fabricates a no-win situation where to receive, the child must always and forever give.

In all these examples, Bruce's, mine, and Ruth's, the cure for the unresolved grief issues is a renewing of the mind. First the emotional process of grief happens and then the more cognitive change in belief systems comes next. Brain studies confirm this. They say that a person must rewire the past experiences by recognizing the present experiences as triggers to the past. They must then process the understanding of how "that was then and this is now" through the more developed cognitive centers of the brain. The feelings invoked by the present situation are applied to the past and seen as fruits of those former times rather than as appropriate reactions to the present. This I believe is one of the ways that we are called to renew our minds with truth. Notice I said that first the emotional process of grief happens. This is because the effectiveness of solely cognitive forms of therapy are being called into question because they don't have this back and forth between the emotional brain and thinking brain that is needed. The left brain, where we hold our belief systems, will not revise those beliefs unless engaged by a relational or emotional event. Those events happen in the right brain and the grieving process uses that part of the brain.

Our Cure Comes from Experiencing God's Presence

I work with people who have been traumatized in various ways through abuse and neglect or simply by living with imperfect people who can never provide love as God meant for us to be loved. Coming to know and appropriate God's presence in their lives wherever they have suffered losses brings healing and a greater communion with God. It also releases the person we were always meant to be in Christ and the power of the Holy Spirit so that we can develop and love others with that love that God our Father has poured out on us.

> **Do not conform any longer to the pattern of this world, but be transformed by the renewing of your mind. Then you will be able to test and approve what God's will is—**
> **his good, pleasing and perfect will.**
> **Romans 12:2**

This procedure for "curing" inappropriate emotional reactions emerged many years ago, in the Word of God through the apostle Paul. You see, we all carry around in our hearts many patterns of this world based on life experiences which we endured without knowing God was with us. Even as a Christian, there may be many moments and situations of our lives where we are totally lacking in faith to believe God is present.

The day I crashed my bike, I was not aware that God was with me. I couldn't see His love for me. All I felt was paralyzing fear. It was only as I revisited that moment via my feelings (triggered by my son learning to ride a bike) that I could experience and apply the truth of God's presence with me. I would like to mention here that people who have an ability to feel God's presence already have an advantage in moving rapidly through the grieving process. Others who can't easily feel Him near need more specialized help to do so.

As for myself, as I dealt with the "bike memory", I also had to recognize it was just the tip of an iceberg representing control problems and my complicity in them. I had been trying to control many things through my life. I had operated out of a type of "hyper-vigilance" in my endeavor to anticipate and manage the constant "dangers" of life. I had to repent of living like an orphan who had only herself to depend upon. Only by identifying this loss, grieving it with God's presence making me safe enough to do so, and turning away from my reactions based on my loss could I have a restoration of my soul. I needed God, not my own protection devices. I was using my own fearfulness to try to protect myself! This was sorrowfully ineffective. Fear leaves and God's perfect love comes in (1 John 4:18) when we choose to let go of trying to keep it all together in our own strength. God is available to those who call on Him.

How many of our present-day reactions and perceptions are embedded in the past? How many moments of godlessness (being without an awareness of God) have we experienced in our lives which need a renewing of the mind? Many more, I think, than we would care to admit. The truth is, we are generally lacking in wisdom concerning these things. We stumble through life deaf, dumb, and blind concerning why we do what we do, or feel what we feel.

> **He who gets wisdom loves his own soul;**
> **he who cherishes understanding prospers.**
> **Proverbs 19:8**

Most of the time, we don't consider that how we view a situation or a person may not be accurate. We don't think about the possibility that we may be interpreting people and events based upon unresolved losses in our past. There is a yearning or desire deep within all of us to reconcile these past losses, to right our past wrongs. This desire is so deeply embedded within us that we often can't isolate it or define it, and can't recognize that it is there.

Understanding this hidden desire and the unresolved losses promoting it, is the key to healing in our current relationships as well as knowing God in all the godless areas of our souls. The examples I have used are not the only types of situations, however, where unresolved losses can be exerting powerful influence upon us. Our sin is closely linked to it. Let me explain.

The world is constantly seeking to explain away sin as an illness. As the modern theory goes, we have been victimized and are not responsible for what we do. At the other extreme are some Christians who reject all psychological techniques and insights, believing that they are of the devil. Everything comes from our sin, they say, and we just need to repent and these sins, by God's help, will all disappear. The concept of unresolved grief shows us a different way of viewing ourselves in relation to our problems, our sin, and their cure, from a deeply Biblical perspective.

Our lives are affected by two types of losses. One type of loss is created by our decisions to do our own thing and leave God out of the picture. The second type of loss involves others' decisions to leave God out of the picture and sin and cause pain and loss to us. On the one hand, Ruth had been rejected and abandoned by her family and had suffered loss at their hands. On the other hand, she spent an enormous amount of energy licking her wounds, expressing anger, and rejecting people around her. This created losses for them as well as for her. The two types of losses in her life were deeply related in that they both were caused by poor decisions contrary to God's way of doing things (He is love). Both losses needed to be reconciled.

The basis of all sin is independence of God. Why can we say this? Because we are all God's creation, created by Him for the express purpose of depending upon Him, having fellowship with Him, and living to accomplish His will for us. What keeps us from fulfilling His purposes is a desire to be independent of God. As we become Christians, by an act of our will, we repent of this independence and begin a long process of surrendering all the areas of our lives to God and His will.

What this means practically, is that whereas we used to strive to meet our own needs in our own power, we now are called by God to look to Him to meet our needs. Therefore, it is a blessed thing, a good thing to be needy and powerless--or to put it in Jesus's own words-- "poor in spirit." If we do so, we are promised to gain the Kingdom of God within us, which is "fullness in Christ". Jesus Christ Himself becomes the way for us to live, the life by which we live it, and the truth that sets us free from our life without God (See John 14:6).

> **But seek first his kingdom and his righteousness,
> and all these things will be given to you as well.
> Matthew 6:33**

It is not a sin to want to be provided for. It is normal and natural to desire food, shelter, safety and a sense of belonging to a group who cares about us. These are appropriate needs that are part of being human. Jesus Christ came and tasted of this humanity and of this neediness. We know he had physical desires because he was hungry and tired and troubled by what he knew he would experience when everyone, especially His Heavenly Father, deserted him. The difference between Jesus and us, however, is that He never attempted to meet these needs outside of God's provision for Him, even though He was tempted to do so. His was a life where He perfectly practiced the presence of God.

He waited on God and depended on God for everything. If something was denied (such as when the Spirit led Him into the desert to fast 40 days), He believed that even His deprivation in the dessert was ordained by God for His purposes. His was a life which had no godlessness. Every one of His human needs was met by the Father. Even in his death He gave himself over to this powerlessness and committed Himself into the hands of the Father. His human flesh was full of the Holy Spirit. There was never any agenda but God's agenda in His thinking, His emotions, and His will.

Ruth needed a different way of relating to people. Theories and standards at a mental level would not change the destructive relational patterns that had plagued her life. She needed to unlearn her ways and learn new ways. A biblical explanation of this is called "dying to the self." It is a letting go of our ways and an embracing of God's way. It is a putting to death the hope that our own protection and control are saving our lives and a relinquishing to God's protection and control. Our way puts us or other people at the center of the universe to make things right. The results of this way in Ruth's life was anger and disappointment towards others, and loneliness and isolation for herself. Her self-protection had not in the end protected her. Her demands that others change their responses to her to make her life right were ruining her relationships. How could Ruth unlearn these ways? How could she die to the self when the self was all she knew?

Our troubles can be a great door of hope for us if we will let them. Allowing ourselves to face loss and grief is the passageway to healing and health.

The grieving process, built into us by God, can turn trouble in our lives around to work for our good. The grieving process allows us to be weaned from our own ways and freed to embrace God's ways. The grief process allows a gradual letting go of "the way it was supposed to be" and opens a door to a new way. Later I will go over more carefully exactly how we grieve and, also, what is necessary to create an environment where grieving will naturally flow. The safety needed for grief comes with an ability to feel God's presence and having assurance we will be loved even when we admit and express negative emotions.

Viewing ourselves or others as the answer to life's problems is a form of idolatry. We turn from idolatry and disengage ourselves from it by moving through the stages of grief. We begin by recognizing that our ways of meeting our own needs are dead and this causes us to let go of them. We admit our powerlessness to establish salvation in our own lives. We admit our wrong at having demanded that others make our lives right. In this place of emptying ourselves of our plans and ambitions, we come to a point of surrendering to God's way and the possibility of emerging into the Divine blueprint already in place within us. Here we let Him comfort us in our grief, change our thinking and show us the lies we have believed as well as the truth we need to set us free.

We who are Christians have a new life given to us in the second birth (being born again) and we are meant to grow in it, re-experiencing the child-like faith that the world and our lives extinguished in us. The Holy Spirit wants to cultivate this life in us. But how does it happen and not just in mere theory? We need to know at the practical level how to die to our life apart from God and relinquish to the life of Christ deposited in us (See also Galatians 2:20).

May God himself, the God of peace,
sanctify you through and through.
May your whole spirit, soul and body be kept blameless

**at the coming of our Lord Jesus Christ.
The one who calls you is faithful and he will do it.
1 Thessalonians 4:10**

The understanding of unresolved grief is true wisdom. Jesus said being little child before God is a prerequisite to entering His kingdom (Matthew 18:1).
This is because children are dependent by nature.

- They are needy, powerless, humble, teachable and willing to trust and make themselves open to relationship.
- They also quickly grieve loss and go on, if allowed.
- They automatically assume that they are unable to meet their own needs and must look to someone else.

This is what is required of us to live in God's kingdom and to have His kingdom flourish and grow in us. Every area of our lives must come to Him in dependency as a little child. (This is total foolishness in the world's eyes, by the way.)

**There is a way that seems right to a man,
but in the end, it leads to death.
Proverbs 14:12**

Remember Ruth's story from the beginning of this booklet? Ruth felt justified in harboring anger and resentment towards others for their reactions to her. She believed she had every right to blame the people around her for her problems. This was a way that seemed right to her, but it ended in death: death to her relationships, death to her hope for change, death to peace.

Ruth needed to face where she had not depended on God and how she had replaced him by faith in herself and others. This could be traced back to her childhood when she was so very powerless and dependent.

It is amazing how easily small children understand this idea. A wonderfully loving friend of mine adopted the three-year-old daughter of a drug addict. Before the adoption was final the child had been moved back and forth between her birth mother and adopted mother two times. A year or so later, the child was watching a television program about an animal that had just given birth to several babies. The babies were being taken from the mother to vaccinate them against disease. At this point in the show, the child became extremely agitated and began to cry out repeatedly, "Don't let them take the babies from the mommy!"

My friend acted in great wisdom at that moment. She gathered the distraught child in her arms and held her tight. She spoke gently to her in this way, "That is what happened to you, isn't it? You were taken from your mommy. That was scary, wasn't it? You must have felt afraid and alone. But now you are safe here with me. Jesus brought you to me to take care of and He will make sure you are safe."

The loving touch and voice of my friend and her assurances of God's presence and love for her child allowed her soul to begin to heal from her traumatic beginnings. As we minister to people, we can do the same thing: be the ambassador of God's love and care for them. He wants to replace all the hurt, fear, and empty places of their lives with His presence, assurance and fullness. Then they can grow into the fullness of the beautiful person He has created them to be.

If you have children, you can be a facilitator of much healing for them by taking their feelings seriously. Loving eye contact, a listening ear and gentle (non-sexual) touch can do wonders to restore your child's soul. Sometimes they just misbehave, but other times their "overreactions" are ways of saying: "I have a loss here that I don't understand and can't resolve." Insight and compassion from us can settle problems now that could otherwise plague them for many years as adults.

It is the losses experienced in our early life and the belief system that emerges from them that affect our adult life. It is our first impressions of self and others that guides our present perceptions and reactions. It is the early experiences that teach us a philosophy of life that may be exceedingly contrary to God's word. But this is where we must begin.

So many Christians take a quantum leap of denial from "the old life" to "the new life in Christ." They expect to pour true spirituality out of a box and into an empty bowl, like freeze dried potato flakes, mix water and stir: poof! A mature, sanctified Christian is created! They fail to realize that Paul wrote his Epistles to believers in whom "Christ was not yet formed".

Our Perceptions, Our Reactions and Our Responses.

So, what are the components of these unresolved grief issues? Unresolved grief is one of the characteristics of what the Bible calls "the flesh" (see Romans 6-8). For it to die, we must first acknowledge it before we can let it go. Our unresolved grief is comprised of three elements: our perceptions, our reactions and our responses.

- Our *Perceptions*: How we see people, events, circumstances.
- Our *Reactions*: How we think and feel about people, events, circumstances.
- Our *Responses*: How we behave or decisions we make in regards to people, events, circumstances.

In other words, why do we see things the way we do (our *perceptions*)? What makes us feel a certain way towards people (our *reactions*)? And why do we then behave the way we do (our *responses)*?

These three components all go back to the underlying belief system within us. Our belief system is that hidden set of rules that we have accepted as true. It is our world view. It is based on the presuppositions from which we make all our interpretations of people, things, and events. Our belief system is our own customized, personalized definition of reality.

Parts of our belief system are known to us, like trusting Jesus as Savior. But other parts are unknown. You may secretly be afraid of people. You may feel unloved and unwanted but have never put that into words. We may be acting on many beliefs which are largely hidden from our awareness.

When our belief system is hidden from our conscious awareness, we will find ourselves repeating certain situations and reactions to those situations over time. At first, we will assume that a force outside of us is causing the problem. But usually by the time we have lived thirty or forty years, we begin to suspect that something is wrong inside of us!

For example, Dave is 45 years old. He has been fired from four jobs over the past fifteen years. He begins each job with a good relationship with his boss and then, when he gets comfortable in his position something always seems to go wrong and he gets fired. Thus, he gets very angry and feels betrayed. The hurt he experiences is so deep that it affects the way he feels about himself as a person. Dave finally, reluctantly agreed to get some help. For the first time, Dave is considering that the unresolved grief issues of his life may be responsible for the unhappy drama that seems to repeat itself. He is finally beginning to look at his belief system and how that was formed and how it is affecting his life.

Dave was the oldest son in a family where the father was an alcoholic. Dave's father was abusive to his mother and the children for many years. Dave believed he had to compensate for his father's shortcomings. He took great initiative for his family and took on tasks well beyond his years. He excelled at most everything he did. Then, when Dave reached puberty, he began to stand up to dad and tried to defend his mother and younger siblings. At this point, Dave came into severe conflict with his father who threw him out of the house. Dave then went to live with an aunt where he finished high school and continued with his life. Since then his father has become a

Christian and stopped drinking. Their relationship is better than it ever has been.

As Dave shared this information with me, he began to see how his job situations had closely paralleled his home life. He'd start out fine at each job with great expectations. Then in time he would notice faults in his company. He would feel betrayed that they were not meeting his high expectations and believe that it was up to him to do something about it. He'd show great initiative and take on tasks well beyond his responsibilities. He'd even openly confront his employer.

As he linked his present feelings to the past hurt from his relationship with his father, Dave began to weep over the way he had felt betrayed by his dad. He felt angry at the abuse and how unjustly his father treated them as a family. He felt the powerlessness of not being able to stop his own pain as well as his mother's and sibling's.

In admitting these feelings, Dave also saw more things about his own belief system. He saw that he felt ashamed of himself as a person. He didn't feel worthwhile unless he was achieving something important. But even then, he still didn't ever feel that what he was doing was important enough. He saw how at work he would threaten his boss by venturing out on his own in his pursuit for significance. This, combined with the mountain of anger he had pent-up against his father, caused him to come off as very aggressive in his endeavors. He finally realized how much he had been contributing to his own dismissals.

I had to help Dave sort through his love/hate relationship with his father. He hated him because he had loved him and hoped for so many good things that never came to pass. Dave addressed his belief system by speaking to his memory of his father like this:

"Dad, I really loved you even though you were mean. Sometimes you were nice to me. I remember you took me fishing and to some ball games. I have been carrying around some hurt and anger toward you that I didn't realize. It's been messing me up at work so I want to deal with it and forgive you for how you hurt me."

"I am angry at you for throwing me out of the house. I was doing the right thing to stand up to you and try to protect Mom. In fact, all the while growing up I was trying to do the right thing to try and win your love. I got good grades in school. I tried hard in sports that you liked, I kept my room clean. Now I see how much of what I did was just to try to please you. But in the end, you rejected me when you kicked me out of the family."

Somewhere in this monologue, Dave starts to cry and his face gets red. Grief sweeps over him and he doubles over with the terrible realization that his initiative and extraordinary efforts as a child were not only an attempt to make up for what his father lacked, but also an attempt to win his dad's affection and approval. These attempts were, in the end, in vain. His hidden belief system has plagued him his entire life, and now for the first time, it is being exposed. So much is making sense from his life. He's finally starting to understand the reason for the pattern in the years of hard work and advancement at different jobs only to end by being booted out the door for the same initiative and drive that caused him to rise in the first place!

Let's trace Dave's path to his unresolved grief issues.

- His *perception* was that he was not loved or cherished.
- His *reaction* to this perception was feelings of rejection, shame and anger.
- His *response* to this perception was that he could somehow earn his father's (or that of any authority figure's) love by performance.

Dave is dazed by how much he has contributed to the way his life has progressed. He sees how angry he has been. He has been in a double bind. He was trying to win the love of those most important to him by his own performance. Yet, in the end, his hard-driving performance-related behaviors drove a wedge between himself and those whose love and respect he desired. The separation from them would cause him to become furious with them that he should ever be in the position to have to earn their favor. On the job, he would channel this anger into ambitious projects, but sooner or later the anger would be directed toward his bosses. All along he found them to be lacking in some way and had then despised them for their weaknesses. Now he was seeing them, as well as himself, in a different light.

Dave spoke again to the memory of his dad: "Dad, I wanted your approval with all my heart. But I see now that you just can't give me what I need. I can no longer demand from my bosses to give me that approval. I can't win their approval and then when they don't seem to give it like I want it, I start to find fault with them because they remind me of you, Dad. You failed me. But, I'm going to cancel the debt you owe me, Dad, because you can never pay it."

At this point, Dave is ready to move away from the sick attachment to his dad and his expectations that have created a life of unresolved grief. His facing the true root of his anger and feeling the sadness and depression of his loss move him towards letting go of what he never got and never will get out of this relationship. He will use the ongoing relationship he has with the Heavenly Father to take the place of everything he wanted and needed from his earthly father. He can thus begin to taste the relationship that was originally meant to happen, before sin:

"Please forgive me, Father, for trying to protect myself with anger. I have hated my father for what he couldn't give me. I have hated men who reminded me of my father. I accept your role as Father and Creator in my life. You created me. You wanted me. You approve of me apart from my performance. You died to pay for my sins while I was still a sinner. You have proven your commitment to me. I see now my dad couldn't give me the perfect love that only You give. I cancel my dad's debt to me. It's not that he wouldn't give it to me. I see now he didn't have it to give. So, I forgive my dad, Lord. And I confess that I have beaten people up with my anger, just like he did to me. I turn from judging him for what I myself have done to others."

Some of this prayer came up automatically from Dave's heart, other parts I coached him as I felt led by the Spirit. But he meant every word of it from his heart. Dave also renounced all the expectations he had put on his bosses and repented of the anger he had dumped on them that was really meant for his father. The sun had gone down on his anger (Ephesians 4:26-27) and Satan had been able to use it to stir up negative reactions in Dave's lifestyle which caused negative consequences in his life.

Such insight broke down an important barrier in Dave. Over time he would then have to break up all the habits of anger and judgment that had formed from these lies. He would need to replace them with the truth of God that is ministered in our lives by the Holy Spirit. Each believer has the constant companionship and help of the Holy Spirit. I encourage them to appropriate this help daily through prayer and practicing the presence of God. Learning to feel Him and hear His voice encouraging us and guiding us can repair our broken inner pieces and lead us in a joyful life full of peace with quick recovery from any future losses. A helpful exercise for connecting to God's perception of us is at firehouseministries.com in the free courses called the "Love and Approval of God" by Richard Kinney.

Short List of Unresolved Grief Issues

Dave is a composite of many people whom I have helped over the years. Observing them and their struggles as well as addressing my own problems, I have compiled a list of what I see as the major unresolved grief issues. The problems arising from these issues plague people's lives until a point comes when they face their need, grieve their loss, and let go of the self-protection measures they employed to guard themselves from loss. Here is my short list of unresolved grief issues.

1. I am not wanted.
2. I have been displaced in my parent's affections by another (or others).
3. I have been abandoned and must take care of myself.
4. I am rejected for who I am.
5. I have been negated as a source of information, particularly about myself and my feelings.

I am not wanted.

Jill imagined before she even met people that they would reject her. So, she avoided others and when she had to interact, she kept up her defenses. Occasionally when the loneliness became unbearable, she would try to say what she thought others wanted to hear. It still left her true self disguised, isolated, and lonely.

Her parents had not wanted any more children, but she arrived when they were in their 40's. Her siblings were all much older and she spent much time alone, entertaining herself. When she did interact with her parents and siblings, she was treated as a bother and not welcomed.

Jill had to face the loss of not being wanted. She needed to face how she had tried to protect herself by rejecting others before they could reject her. She also had to look at her way of being phony to try to please others and win their favor. She had put a defensive layer around herself to guarantee no rejection could enter. This, unfortunately, protected her too well. It also kept out any positive advances others might have tried to make to get to know her. She contributed to the fulfillment of her belief that she was not wanted.

I have been displaced in my parent's affections by another (or others).

Jack was the leader of a small Christian ministry. Jack couldn't stand anyone competing with his ministry. He always felt deeply insulted by people not recognizing or contributing to his ministry. He believed it was one of a kind, better than others and worthy of the attention of other Christians far and wide. He truly believed there must be something wrong with them that they didn't acknowledge the wisdom and power of God working through his ministry. He would have his prayer group pray and ask God to convince pastors and church leaders to recognize and desire to include his ministry in their programs and support it.

He constantly mentored people to work with him, but when his helpers became successful, Jack found a reason to dismiss them. He would constantly choose some person to be his favorite, telling them he would hone them to replace him and take over the ministry when he was gone. But when they began to show promise and develop their giftings, he always found fault with them. He even confessed to one of them "When you are up front I don't feel special anymore." It never occurred to him that he was envious of the talent and success of others.

Jack had to compete with many siblings growing up. He had to constantly prove his point and convince others that he was right and should be heard. He wanted to feel special. He worked hard everywhere he went to gain attention and be recognized. This ministry was something that could distinguish him from the others. Jack never recognized his striving and diligent work ethic as a desperate endeavor to gain the favor of his parents. He had covered his unresolved grief issues with a lifetime of hard work, sacrifice and worst of all, the image that all he was doing was really for God and others. He truly believed he was justified in bullying others to promote his ministry. After all, it was "God's ministry" and almost any means justified the ends of making His ministry successful.

I have been abandoned and must take care of myself.

Judy always had to make sure that no one was picking up the slack for her. She would refuse to ask for help because it was a great embarrassment to need others. The thought of exposing herself as weak or dependent made her feel ill. She was constantly caring for friends and family but never letting anyone know when she needed help. Every holiday and family get-together was at her house and she bore the brunt of most of the work. At the same time, Judy was backing anyone off from helping her, she wondered why no one seemed to care about her needs. She resented having all the work "dumped" on her and secretly held strong hostility for everyone she "sacrificially" helped. Unfortunately, she never saw herself as the problem.

She truly believed that others were just being selfish and that eventually they would be won over by her good modeling of selfless service. She had been waiting for others to change for twenty years and, so far, no one had.

Judy was the middle child in a needy family. She decided at a young age to try and fill in all the gaps that were lacking in her parents. She cared for younger siblings and tried to be a friend to both her parents. She was an honor student and often cooked and cleaned for her mother. She helped her father find a rehab for her older brother. Judy had been in an incubator as an infant. She fought back from near death as a premature baby. She had a big heart and great courage, but from those earliest days the enemy of her soul had caught her in a horrible lie: I must take care of myself and strive to make my world safe. She couldn't see that even as a child her hard work to make the family better was really the concentrated effort to create a protected, orderly living space for herself.

I am rejected for who I am.

Dean had only one memory from his childhood. He was standing in his crib waiting for someone or something to happen, he wasn't sure what. The next thing he remembered was in junior high and liking a girl. He tried on several occasions to speak to her but she looked at him as if he were weird. In conversations, Dean always talked about superficial things: sports, cars, weather and girl's bodies. He had totally lost contact with his real heart and desires and longings. By twenty he had decided that sex was the answer to whatever he needed. He had no ability to form any kind of lasting relationships or friendships. His idea of success was to find someone to sleep with. Even while he pursued this lifestyle he felt great shame about it. He had given his heart to Christ as a teen at a special concert he attended with a friend. A small voice kept trying to get his attention. Finally, one day he listened to it and began to try and remember something from his childhood. He wanted to find that part of himself that could hope and care about others.

He called his mother, something he hadn't done in months and asked her some questions about his early life. His father had died when he was a year old. His mother immediately went to work and left him in a day care. His mother began to cry as she confessed that Dean so reminded her of his father that she couldn't bear to be with him. He spent endless hours at the day care and even when that was over she often left him at her sister's. Dean's mother gave him a key that day, a key to help him understand the pattern of his life. Besides feeling abandoned by his parents, he had also internalized the terrible lie that something about him was "detestable." His childlike understanding couldn't sort out the family tragedy or that his mother rejected him because of his resemblance to his father. All he knew was that he was rejected, unwanted by the person whom he needed most.

> I have been negated as a source of information, particularly about myself and my feelings.

Dawn had to give up her job. She was heavily medicated with several drugs to keep her from killing herself. For years, she had suffered depression and anxiety. She wondered if she would have to move back home with her parents. That would not be easy. Her mother was a difficult person to keep happy. Even when away from her mother Dawn could constantly hear "tapes" in her head of mother's advice and rebukes. The confusing thing was that sometimes mother's tapes would contradict each other.

"Life is short, so eat and drink and enjoy life."
"Watch out what you eat or you'll get fat."
"Why are you refusing to eat this meal I worked so hard to make? Are you trying to reject me?"
"Why are you always busy and running around doing errands instead of spending time with me?"
"Why are you always idle—sitting and staring at me? Can't you find something to keep yourself occupied?"

Dawn felt that her mother owned her life. She made her take vitamins and drink horrible juices. Her mother seemed to know better than her when she was tired, afraid, depressed or in need. Dawn strangely felt inhabited by her mother.

As a child, Dawn tried to comply with her mother. She felt closer to her mother than anyone else. If Mom said to "have fun" then she would dance and sing and try to look happy. If Mom was in a bad mood, Dawn would try to cheer her up. Her highly sensitive nature was constantly in tune to Mom's feelings. At around thirteen years old, Dawn tried to make other friends but her mother always convinced her that there was something wrong with them. Dawn was afraid of people and these warnings confirmed her fears. So, she stayed alone. Finally, when she could stand the aloneness no longer, she joined a writing club at school. One day a week she would meet with a small group of students and read each other's poems and essays. This enraged her mother but Dawn loved the club so much she couldn't bring herself to quit.

Suddenly, her mother became exceedingly hostile to Dawn. Whereas for years the mother has praised Dawn for being the perfect child, now nothing she did seemed to be right. The way she dressed, the ways she walked and styled her hair were all silly. Dawn went from being brilliant to stupid, in her mother's eyes.

Unable to see anything wrong with her mother, Dawn began to wonder what terrible thing had happened to her to so quickly turn her into such a monster. She began to spiral into a deep depression. This brought more negative commentary from her mother. Before long, not only did Dawn quit her writing club but school as well. A tutor came to her home and helped her to complete her junior year. Her aloneness again set in.

Soon Dawn lost interest in most things. Around this time her mother stopped the constant criticism. But now she began telling her family and friends that Dawn was probably crazy and needed medicine. She took Dawn to a specialist who prescribed several different medicines. At the same time, Dawn's mother gave her daughter her meds, she would berate her and claim that she herself never had to deal with her problems through drugs. Dawn would just nod her head and swallow the pills.

Dawn left home against the wishes of her mother. She felt better when she was alone. She got a job as a data entry clerk. Sometimes while falling asleep at night she would remember her poetry and writing and long to share it with someone. But who could she trust? People were scary. Finally, the job was even too much for Dawn's fragile mental condition. Now she was faced with the dilemma of having to return home.

Hope for Dawn could only begin by a separation from her mother's feelings and viewpoint. She had used her mother as an absolute in her life. The ruler she used to measure herself and her life was terribly twisted and bent. No wonder Dawn was caught in mixed messages and despair. Her mother had been her "god" who in the end wasn't meeting her needs. Serving her mother had left her depressed, anxious, suicidal, and without meaning.

Dawn needed a new absolute, the real God. Sadly, many people with Dawn's background find churches that also negate them as a source of information about themselves. Almost cult-like, some sick church systems encourage people to try to forget their humanness and live in a superficial realm of religious platitudes and pat answers.

Here are some other common unresolved grief issues:

1. I have been ignored, particularly my true self.
2. My needs for approval, attention, affection, self-worth, belonging, connection, etc. have been neglected.
3. I have been abused physically, emotionally or sexually.

4. I have been used as a surrogate parent instead of being allowed to be a child.
5. I have never been noticed, the real me seems to be invisible.
6. I am noticed but I am despised.
7. I fluctuate between being noticed and despised, and being invisible.

It is truly amazing to me how people recreate these losses in their adult lives until they are resolved. Recently someone came to me with the following "problem": she only liked her husband when he was off traveling. We asked for the presence of the Lord Jesus to come to us and show us where this pattern began in her life. She remembered her father had left to go to war when she was young. She had dreamed about what it would be like if only he were home. This comforted her while he was gone, but when he returned, his brusque and callous attitude towards her destroyed her fantasy. We asked the Lord Jesus who is the same yesterday, today, and forever to take her back to the feelings she had at this young age in her life. At this point, my friend began to cry and say she felt very afraid. I allowed her to cry for a little while and then I had her say: "Lord Jesus, I am very afraid. I need a father but my father doesn't seem to know how to love me. I need you to love me."

We then discussed how she had shut out her husband with a hefty dose of anger left over from her relationship with her father. She repented of using this to protect herself from the pain and loss of having felt abandoned by her father emotionally. We asked Jesus to come to her in this place and prayed for all footholds of the enemy in this area of her soul to leave. We discussed what "habits" she would have to break, with the help of the Holy Spirit, to change her attitude and actions towards her husband.

Because she was willing to face this loss and grieve it, she resolved it by letting go of her answer to her need and receiving the love of Christ and His fullness in that place. An infilling of Christ and communion with him is essential for change. Sometimes people will spend years hardening themselves to their losses. Even though they have avoided the pain of the loss they have not avoided effects of the loss. It still insidiously infuses a silent theme into their lives that they can't escape.

Others of a more emotional sort will spend much time crying and raging over their losses, but not really resolving them because they are not willing to face how they have protected themselves and cooperated with a lie. Some just don't have enough faith to trust God to give them what they lack. Ultimately, another relationship is needed to replace what was needed but never provided during our past. We will either surrender ourselves into the arms of God to give us that relationship, or we will continue to replicate broken relationships to try to resolve our issues ourselves.

Living Like an Orphan

Many people over the years have come to me with a similar problem: they did not feel wanted by their parents and so they have behaved as an orphan. One woman, Monica, had a rather stable and loving family. But when her parents were both in college they were at first dismayed by an unwanted pregnancy but their disappointment quickly faded when Monica was born. But Monica's lasting perception of her parents was based on the temporary disappointment. Her reaction to this perception was a deep-down belief that no one wanted her, that she was a bother and needed to provide for herself. Basically, she felt like an orphan. Her response towards her parents was to hold herself aloof and distant. She didn't like to let them do things for her. She barely asked for anything even though her parents were willing to give to her. Though she didn't need to, Monica lived like an orphan. She embraced a lie formed in the womb and by her reaction to it and response to others; she helped to create an environment around her that further encouraged the perception that she was truly an orphan. Her mind wrestled with this scenario. Objective facts told her that her parents were good people who seemed to love her. But deep in her heart another reality was raging that created constant loneliness and disappointment and a terrible sense of not being wanted. Only in uncovering the lie she embraced from the womb and grieving the losses created by her responses to that lie could she be set free from her self-inflicted prison.

Another man, Bob, was the first child after his mother had a series of miscarriages. Bob was convinced that life was not worth living and had tried to commit suicide several times. Somehow, he had perceived that his mother's womb was a place of death and felt guilty that he had lived while his siblings had died. He was reacting to a lie that said everything was his fault. His mother's problems were somehow because of him. He imagined other people to be victimized by his very existence. His response was to try to redeem the mistake of his life by taking it. The only way to live, Bob thought, was to die.

I believe many people who are caught in destructive addictions have a similar belief system to Bob's. Life seems like a game that they can never win. For Bob, deliverance came as a series of acceptances that he had played God over his own life and needed to accept God's will that he should live. I helped him to grieve the loss of all those siblings who died before him. I assured him they were in heaven waiting to meet him when God decided he should go. Bob also had to grieve the fact that he didn't have control over or responsibility for everyone else's feelings. He came to see that viewing everything as his fault was a way of avoiding powerlessness and a way of staying in control. If everything was his fault, then he was in the driver's seat. He didn't have to count on anyone else to give him significance. He viewed himself as having great significance, albeit negative significance. But negative significance was viewed as better than no significance at all. He was at the center of his world.

I am sure that no book or booklet can contain all the different ways that human beings have suffered losses or reacted to their losses. When we accept that we were created to live in a perfect world in unbroken communion with God, our sufferings come into a different light. I hear people trying to shame those who openly try to grieve their losses, saying such things as: "Oh, you don't know what suffering is! Think of those people in countries where they are in prison for their faith. And what about all the starving, homeless people in the third world?"

Let's look at that line of reasoning briefly. So, because I have judged other's pain greater than my own, I have no right to admit that I am hurting or that my pain has validity? Only the "worst" case scenarios are true losses. This requires a hardening of heart towards what are considered "minor" losses. That results in a refusal to feel pain because the mind can't justify a serious enough reason for it. This also ends up being a defense mechanism to avoid pain.

Recognizing the sick patterns of our lives is the first step towards being healed of them. Taking responsibility for our choices based on our losses and grieving them is the next important milestone in this process. By facing our losses directly, grieving them and then seeking the face of God and inviting his Presence where we have had loss is the true point of healing for all our lacks. He is our Shepherd and because of that we will not stay in need. Here is a prayer you can start with in your journey to know God. Sit and quiet yourself each day and ask the Holy Spirit to help you receive God's love and perspective.

"Heavenly Father, I don't have all that I need. I have tried many ways to get what I need on my own but have failed to satisfy my soul. Jesus experienced humanity so He could understand and help me. Please come to me now and give me His life and help through the Holy Spirit. Help me to let go of my own perceptions and demands. Help me to have faith to trust you to take care of me. Thank you for your promise that you will never leave me or forsake me. No matter what losses I have had in life, always let me finish in Your Divine Embrace as I let them go. In Jesus name, Amen."

Bibliography

Benner, David B. *Soulful Spirituality.* Grand Rapids, MI: Brazos Press, 2011.

Benner, David G. *The Gift of Being Yourself, The Sacred Call to Self Discovery.* Downer's Grove, Illinois: IVP Books, 2004.

Bozarth, A. *Life is Goodbye, Life is hello: Grieving Well Through All Kind of Loss.* Minneapolis, MN: CompCare Publications, 1986.

Brison, Stephen Leavitt and Karen. "Coping with Bereavement: Long-Term Perspectives on Grief and Mourning." *Ethos*, 1995: 365.

Campbell, Dr. Ross. *How to Really Love Your Child.* Colorado Springs: David C. Cook, 1977.

Coursey, E. James Wilder and Chris M. *Share Immanuel, The Healing Lifestyle.* Pasadena, CA: Shepherd's House Inc., 2010.

E. James Wilder, et. al. *Joy Starts Here.* Pasadena, CA: Shepherd's House Inc., 2013.

Goleman, Daniel. *Emotional Intelligence.* New York: Bantam Books, 1994.

James E. Friesen, et. al. *The Life Model, Living Out of the Heart Jesus Gave You.* Pasadena, CA: Shepherd's House Inc., 2000.

Karl Lehman, M.D. *Outsmarting Yourself.* Libertyville, IL: This JOY! Books, 2011.

Kubler-Ross, Karen. *On Death and Dying.* New York: Touchstone, 1969.

Lauback, Frank, and Brother Lawrence. *Practicing His Presence.* Jacksonville, FL: Seed Sowers, n.d.

Leman, Dr. Kevin, and Dr. Kevin Carlson. *Unlocking the Secrets of Your Childhood Memories.* Nashville, TN: Thomas Nelson, Inc., 1989.

Mendez, Dr. Mario E. Rivera. *Emotional Freedom.* Green Forest, AZ: New Leaf Press, 1992.

—. *Pulling Down Hang-ups.* Green Forest, AZ: New Leaf Press, 1988.

Miller, Alice. *Banished Knowledge.* New York: Doubleday, 1990.

—. *For Your Own Good.* New York: The Noonday Press, 1990.

Wilder, E. James. *The Complete Guide to Living with Men.* Pasadena, CA: Shepherd's House Inc., 2004.

Made in the USA
Columbia, SC
09 September 2018